NAPOLEON, FRANCE
and EUROPE

2nd Edition

Andrina Stiles
and
Dylan Rees

Hodder & Stoughton

A MEMBER OF THE HODDER HEADLINE GROUP

The publishers would like to thank the following individuals, institutions and companies for permission to reproduce copyright illustrations in this book:

© Archivo Iconographico, S.A./CORBIS: pages 121, 142 (bottom); © Bettman/CORBIS: pages 14, 37; © Bridgeman Art Library/National Museums and Galleries on Merseyside: page 142 (top); © The British Library: page 82; © The British Museum: page 16; © Mansell/Time Life Pictures/Getty Images: page 143.

Every effort has been made to trace and acknowledge ownership of copyright. The publishers will be glad to make suitable arrangements with any copyright holders whom it has not been possible to contact.

Papers used in this book are natural, renewable and recyclable products. They are made from wood grown in sustainable forests. The logging and manufacturing processes conform to the environmental regulations of the country of origin.

Orders: please contact Bookpoint Ltd, 130 Milton Park, Abingdon, Oxon OX14 4SB. Telephone: (44) 01235 827720. Fax: (44) 01235 400454. Lines are open from 9.00–6.00, Monday to Saturday, with a 24 hour message answering service. You can also order through our website www.hodderheadline.co.uk.

British Library Cataloguing in Publication Data
A catalogue record for this title is available from the British Library

ISBN 0 340 84582 1

First Published 2004
Impression number   10 9 8 7 6 5 4 3 2 1
Year   2010 2009 2008 2007 2006 2005 2004

Copyright © Andrina Stiles, Dylan Rees 2004

Cover illustration shows a portrait of Napoleon by Ingres (Courtesy Musée de Liege/Bridgeman Art Library)
Produced by Gray Publishing, Tunbridge Wells, Kent
Printed in Great Britain for Hodder & Stoughton Educational, a division of Hodder Headline, 338 Euston Road, London NW1 3BH by The Bath Press, Bath

Contents

Preface

To the general reader

Although the *Access to History* series has been designed with the needs of students studying the subject at higher examination levels very much in mind, it also has a great deal to offer the general reader. The main body of the text (i.e. ignoring the 'Study Guides' at the end of each chapter) forms a readable and yet stimulating survey of a coherent topic as studied by historians. However, each author's aim has not merely been to provide a clear explanation of what happened in the past (to interest and inform): it has also been assumed that most readers wish to be stimulated into thinking further about the topic and to form opinions of their own about the significance of the events that are described and discussed (to be challenged). Thus, although no prior knowledge of the topic is expected on the reader's part, she or he is treated as an intelligent and thinking person throughout. The author tends to share ideas and possibilities with the reader, rather than passing on numbers of so-called 'historical truths'.

To the student reader

This title ensures the results of recent research are reflected in the text and includes features aimed at assisting you in your study of the topic at AS Level, A Level and Higher. Two features are designed to assist you during your first reading of a chapter. The *Points to consider* section following each chapter title is intended to focus your attention on the main theme(s) of the chapter, and the issues box following most section headings alerts you to the question or questions to be dealt with in the section. The *Working on ...* section at the end of each chapter suggests ways of gaining maximum benefit from the chapter.

There are many ways in which the series can be used by students studying History at a higher level. It will, therefore, be worthwhile thinking about your own study strategy before you start work on this book. Obviously, your strategy will vary depending on the aim you have in mind, and the time for study that is available to you.

If, for example, you want to acquire a general overview of the topic in the shortest possible time, the following approach will probably be the most effective:

1 Read Chapter 1. As you do so, keep in mind the issues raised in the *Points to Consider* section.

2   Read the *Points to Consider* section at the beginning of Chapter 2 and decide whether it is necessary for you to read this chapter.

3   If it is, read the chapter, stopping at each heading or sub-heading to note down the main points that have been made. Often, the best way of doing this is to answer the question(s) posed in the *Key issues* boxes.

4   Repeat stage 2 (and stage 3 where appropriate) for all the other chapters.

If, however, your aim is to gain a thorough grasp of the topic, taking however much time is necessary to do so, you may benefit from carrying out the same procedure with each chapter, as follows:

1   Try to read the chapter in one sitting. As you do this, bear in mind any advice given in the *Points to Consider* section.

2   Study the flow diagram at the end of the chapter, ensuring that you understand the general 'shape' of what you have just read.

3   Read the *Working on ...* section and decide what further work you need to do on the chapter. In particularly important sections of the book, this is likely to involve reading the chapter a second time and stopping at each heading and sub-heading to think about (and probably to write a summary of) what you have just read.

4   Attempt the *Source-based questions* section. It will sometimes be sufficient to think through your answers, but additional understanding will often be gained by forcing yourself to write them down.

When you have finished the main chapters of the book, study the *Further reading* section and decide what additional reading (if any) you will do on the topic.

This book has been designed to help make your studies both enjoyable and successful. If you can think of ways in which this could have been done more effectively, please contact me. In the meantime, I hope that you will gain greatly from your study of History.

Robert Pearce

1 Napoleon: An Introductory Overview

POINTS TO CONSIDER

This chapter aims at providing you with a brief overview of Napoleon's career and some of the main historical issues which students *need* to be aware of. The opening section provides general biographical detail which seeks to map out Napoleon's background, character and personality, before considering some general features of his rule in France and Europe. You should consider carefully the significant and key points of Napoleon's life which are outlined here, and ensure that you are familiar with them before proceeding.

KEY DATES

1769	**August**	Born at Ajaccio on the island of Corsica
1784		Entered *Ecole Militaire* Paris
1785		Commissioned as artillery officer
1793		In command of artillery at siege of Toulon
1796	**February**	Appointed commander of army in Italy
1798	**May**	Embarks for Egypt
1799	**November**	*Coup* of Brumaire
	December	Appointed *First Consul*
1804	**May**	Proclaimed Emperor of the French
1809	**December**	Divorces Josephine
1810	**April**	marriage to Marie-Louise of Austria
1811	**March**	Birth of son, the King of Rome
1814	**April**	Abdication by Napoleon
1815	**March**	Escapes from Elba and attempts to regain power
	June	Defeat at Waterloo, second abdication
	October	Exile to St Helena in the south Atlantic
1821	**5 May**	Death of Napoleon, burial at St Helena
1840	**December**	Remains exhumed and reburied at *Les Invalides* in Paris

A new calendar and dating system was adopted by the French Republic in October 1793 to mark what it considered was a new era in human history. Year I started in September 1792 when the Republic came into existence. The second month in the new revolutionary calendar was Brumaire – the month of fog. On 18–19 Brumaire in the year VIII of the Revolution (9–10 November 1799) a *coup d'état* in Paris unexpectedly brought a young General, Napoleon Bonaparte, to power in France. In the event it also led to him assuming power in most of the rest of Europe during the course of the next 15 years.

Who was he and what was he like, this man who was to dominate Europe until 1815, and to live on in the legend after his death?

1 Background and Character

> **KEY ISSUES** What was Napoleon's background and character? What was his early military career? How was he able to progress up the ranks?

On 15 August 1769 at Ajaccio on the island of Corsica Napoleon was born a French subject, but only just, for Corsica had been part of the Republic of Genoa until the previous year when it was ceded to France. The Buonaparte family was petty nobility with a fierce, independent pride in all that was Corsican, and at first Napoleon's father was a bitter opponent of the foreign French occupation. Before long, though, he accepted an amnesty and changed sides, seeing advantages to be gained for his growing family of five sons and three daughters by attaching himself to the French administration of the island. One of the advantages he obtained was the documentary proof of nobility he needed in order to send Napoleon, his second son, to be educated at the French government's expense at a military academy on the mainland. Fortunately perhaps for Napoleon, the Corsican nobility was considered by most Frenchmen to be much inferior in status to that of France, and his name was never entered in the '*ci-devant*' (former aristocrat) lists at the time of the Revolution.

Strictly speaking, Napoleon should, prior to becoming Emperor in 1804, be referred to simply as Bonaparte, or General Bonaparte. It was not until 1802 that his full name appeared for the first time in official documents, when it was given as 'Napoleone Bonaparte'. (He had much earlier abandoned the Italian spelling of his surname, Buonaparte.) Soon after 1802 the Italian version of his baptismal name was also dropped, in favour of the French, Napoléon. It was to be a source of conflict with his British gaolers on St Helena that, having been deprived by the Allies of his imperial title at the time of his second abdication in 1815, they addressed their prisoner as 'General Bonaparte'. The argument continued even after his death in a very undignified way. The British officials on the island would not agree to the name 'Napoléon' being put on the coffin, and as the French representatives there would accept nothing else, he was buried anonymously. (For the sake of simplicity, Napoleon, the anglicised form of his name, is used throughout this book.)

At the age of nine the young Napoleon, whose first language was Italian, was given a crash course in French to prepare him for his future career. He never lost his Italian accent, though, and never learnt to write French grammatically – this latter fact may have been an unadmitted reason why he always dictated official documents and correspondence leaving it to his secretaries to correct the grammar. It is difficult to know how far he ever felt himself to be truly French, however much he spoke of 'France, first and always'. Some historians go so far as to suggest that France for him was never *la patrie* – that he was always, at least emotionally, a Corsican. It is certainly true that he initially thought of the Revolution as an opportunity for the Corsicans to gain freedom from France as they had once dreamed of gaining freedom from Genoa. During the opening years of the revolution Napoleon was very influenced by the philosopher Rousseau who developed a theory of popular sovereignty whereby ordinary people would exercise political power. For a while he was obsessed with Rousseau's 'presentiment that this little island will one day astonish Europe'.[1] Later, when Corsica ceased to dominate his thoughts in the same way and he had denounced Rousseau as 'a madman', the Corsican sense of family loyalty remained with him.

Napoleon studied first at a preparatory school in France, before going on to the École Militaire in Paris where he became the first Corsican to graduate, as a sub-lieutenant of artillery in 1785. For the next four years he continued his training as an artillery officer, while at the same time managing to spend a good deal of time in Corsica. During this period he came to the notice of an influential politician, Paul Barras, whose patronage undoubtedly helped his early career, and whose mistress, Josephine, Napoleon later married. In the years between 1789 and 1792, with the emigration of as many as 6000 noble commissioned officers, there were plenty of opportunities for able and energetic, but not particularly well-born or well-endowed, career-soldiers to advance rapidly up the ladder of promotion in a way undreamed of under the *ancien régime*. A whole-hearted supporter of the Revolution from its beginning in 1789, Napoleon was one of the ambitious young men to be quickly promoted. Much is made of his meteoric rise. In reality 'His experience of the revolutionary years might best be described as not untypical in an exceptional era'.[2] Lucien, Napoleon's younger brother carved out for himself a successful political career through his own exertions. Napoleon's role in helping to recapture the port of Toulon in 1793 resulted in his promotion at the age of 24 to the rank of brigadier-general. In the same year he published a pamphlet that was very sympathetic to the extreme Jacobin government whose leading figure was Maximilian Robespierre. This brought him to the notice of Augustine Robespierre, Maximilian's brother. In a letter to his brother Augustine mentioned favourably the young soldier:

I add to the names of patriots I have already mentioned citizen Buonoparte, general in command of artillery, a man of transcendent merit. He is Corsican, and brings me the simple guarantee of a man of that country who resisted the blandishments of Paoli [a leading Corsican nationalist soldier whom Napoleon had once admired] and whose property has been destroyed by that traitor.[3]

Napoleon's character was a complex one. With friends he could be charming and amusing – 'no one could be more fascinating, when he chose'. But he did not always choose, and his rages and his cold displeasure could be terrifying to those around him. He recognised the fact that his mood could change suddenly: 'I am two different men', he once said of himself. One of his most perceptive biographers, Georges Lefebvre, pointed out that the young Napoleon possessed an '… irresistible impulse towards action and domination which is called ambition'.[4] Napoleon himself clearly recognised and fully acknowledged this trait: 'It is said that I am ambitious, but that is an error: or at least, my ambition is so intimately allied to my whole being that it cannot be separated from it.'

It is a historical cliché that Napoleon was unusually short – the 'Little Corporal' of contemporary cartoons – and that his superabundant energy and overweening ambition are explained by a need to compensate for his lack of inches. Energetic and ambitious he may have been, but at a time when the standard height for adult enrolment in the French army was 5 feet (approximately 150 cm), reduced by 1813 to 4 feet 9 inches (approximately 142 cm), Napoleon at 5 feet 2 inches (approximately 155 cm) was in fact above average height for a Frenchman. Very intelligent and full of vitality, he was, for much of his adult life, a workaholic, sometimes working 18 or more hours a day. His handwriting was indecipherable – it could not, he said, keep up with his thoughts so fast did ideas come to him – and he normally dictated his official communications to a half a dozen secretaries at once. It has been estimated that he 'wrote' more than 80,000 documents during his 15 years in power. Because he lived on his nerves he sometimes became anxious and fearful – especially in crowds, or when called upon to speak in public (which he did very badly). At such times he seems to have suffered from nervous collapses akin to epilepsy.

In 1796 after winning the battle of Lodi during his first Italian campaign he realised, he said, that he was a superior being destined to perform great things, and this belief in his 'destiny' remained with him as a driving force. He openly acknowledged that his ambition was unlimited. Whether it was as he often said ambition for France, to make her feared, respected and ruler of the world, or whether it was a similar ambition for himself, remains a matter of dispute. Military historians vary in their judgement of Napoleon's abilities as a general, but whatever the verdict on his strategy and tactics, there is no doubt about his charismatic powers of leadership.

From 1807 onwards officials, friends and servants noticed a change in Napoleon, which became more marked after the return from

Moscow in 1812. The Russian campaign seemed to have affected both his mental and physical health. Although only 43 in 1812 his previously excellent memory began to decline, he became more imperious and intolerant of others' points of view and more brutally contemptuous of the rest of the human race – 'Power comes through fear', he said at this time. He began to put on weight, becoming lethargic and slow, and ageing prematurely into the balding, paunchy figure beloved of cartoonists then and since.

2 Synopsis of Career: 1796–1815

> **KEY ISSUE** What are the main features of Napoleon's rule?

At the beginning of his ascent to power in the 1790s, Napoleon was still slim and active, although not particularly prepossessing in appearance according to eyewitness accounts. These describe him as untidily, almost shabbily dressed, with lank, greasy shoulder-length hair and a sallow complexion. A rather serious young man, he had little sense of humour and seldom laughed. In March 1796 two events of great importance in his life occurred – he married the widowed society beauty, Josephine de Beauhearnais, and he was appointed commander of the Army of Italy. It was as a result of his military successes in Italy (1796–7) and afterwards in Egypt (1798–9) that in 1799 he came to power in the *coup d'état* of Brumaire, making him *First Consul* and undisputed ruler of France.

i) Domestic Affairs

As *First Consul* (1799–1804) and then as Emperor until 1814, Napoleon's government was highly centralised and his authority as sole ruler of France was not effectively disputed. His régime was basically a dictatorship, although, despite the fact that the head of state was also head of the armed forces, it was not a military one. By a mixture of bribery (through the liberal use of gifts of land, titles, official appointments and money to buy support) and a ruthless suppression of freedom of thought, word and deed (through the equally liberal use of indoctrination, intimidation and propaganda to make opposition difficult), Napoleon maintained himself in power for 14 years.

ii) Foreign Affairs

Foreign affairs for Napoleonic France were indistinguishable from war. Apart from the short period of peace in 1802–3 France was almost continuously at war under Napoleon. Indeed, the Peace of Amiens (1802) can be seen as little more than a truce in a long succession of wars begun under the Revolution and continued under Napoleon, which were fought by France against a succession of European coalition armies. Until 1807 Napoleon led France to a series of brilliant victories on land, extending the French frontiers far beyond their 'natural' limits of the Rhine, the Alps and the Pyrenees, into Germany and Italy. At the beginning of 1811 the Empire reached its greatest extent, but its collapse was already threatened by the lengthy Spanish conflict begun in 1807 and made certain by the ill-judged invasion of Russia in 1812. Even Napoleon's most strenuous efforts failed to save the Empire in the campaign of 1813 and with the fall of Paris to the Allies in March 1814 he was forced to abdicate, and was exiled to Elba (an island off the Italian coast). His return to France the following year (the Hundred Days) and his defeat at Waterloo marked the end of his public life.

iii) St Helena and After

Exiled again in 1815, this time to St Helena (a remote island in the south Atlantic from which escape proved impossible), Napoleon occupied the remaining years of his life in dictating his own version of events to a group of companions on the island. He died, most probably from stomach cancer, in 1821 shortly before his 52nd birthday. From these records, and from the accumulated propaganda of his years in power, his many followers carefully constructed the Napoleonic legend.

3 Historical Issues

> **KEY ISSUE** How has Napoleon's rule been interpreted since his death?

This book is concerned with Napoleon's rise and fall; with the military, political, social, cultural and economic effects, both long term and short term, on those who came under his control at home and abroad; with the reasons for his success and eventual failure; his relationship with the French Revolution and with the development of the 'Napoleonic legend'.

He was the supreme egoist: 'Himself is the only man he recognises – all other beings are mere cyphers', as one who knew him well remarked. Self-interest, he freely admitted, was his guide in all things. No one could deflect him from his plans – not even his first wife, Josephine, who was probably the only person he ever loved apart from himself. Contemporaries regarded him as amoral, a man to whom the labels good or bad were not applicable, who felt neither love nor hate, and who dispensed favours and kindness only in proportion to the usefulness of the recipient. He was not personally cruel – merely indifferent to the sufferings of others. They were only of value as they served his purpose – expendable when they did not. Why he lavished so much largesse on his mostly unpleasant and ungrateful relatives – he made four brothers and three brothers-in-law into kings or princes – is not entirely clear. It may have been an expression of his dynastic ambition to found a European royal house of Bonaparte to rival the Habsburgs who ruled over Austria and outshine the overthrown French royal family the Bourbons; possibly it was the Corsican sense of family clannishness that never left him. Nor did the Corsican tradition of the vendetta, which he called upon to justify – at least to himself – the judicial murder in 1804 of the Duc d'Enghien, who was said to have been involved in a plot to assassinate him.

For two centuries novelists, biographers, artists, playwrights, and lately film-makers, have all found material for their talents in depicting the life and times of Napoleon. Their views on him have usually been unsubtly polarised – the great soldier and strong ruler unjustly exiled, or the evil dictator well nicknamed the 'Ogre' and deservedly banished. Until after the Second World War even historians, caught up in the old historical assumption that events were dictated almost exclusively by the actions of powerful personalities – the 'great man' school of thought – concentrated on analysing Napoleon's personal contribution to European history, and declared it to have been either 'good' or 'bad'. This is very clearly brought out by the Dutch historian Pieter Geyl in his 'for and against' synthesis of the views of nineteenth and early twentieth century French historians on Napoleon's achievements.[5] All of them based their conclusions on detailed studies of Napoleon, the man. This in itself presented a problem, for it can be argued that there were two Napoleons – the living one and the one of the legend. Chapter 8 of this book looks at the legend, how it developed and how far, if at all, it can be taken at face value.

With a lessening of interest in the personal aspects of Napoleon's career, historical research on the period has moved since the 1960s into other areas. As a result, doubt has been cast on a number of long-cherished beliefs. In important reassessments of Napoleon as a soldier it has been shown that he was by no means deserving of the title of 'the greatest military leader of all time' that has so often been accorded to him. Many of his campaigns were bungled and his success dependent on the even greater incompetence of his enemies. Recent investigations into the social, cultural and economic history of the period have suggested that there was a much greater continuity with the past than was once thought, and that the extent of changes in Napoleonic society in France and in the Empire has been exaggerated. In the same way the idea of Napoleon as a radical reformer in his early domestic policies (the 'Consular miracle' of 1800–2) has come in for considerable reappraisal.

One of the great difficulties for English-speaking students studying the Napoleonic period was the limited availability of the most recent and up-to-date research by French historians. As Geoffrey Ellis pointed out, we are largely 'isolated from the mainstream of current Napoleonic research abroad ... Our knowledge and understanding of Napoleon's impact on France and on Europe remains old-fashioned, lop-sided and is now increasingly mistaken. So far from coming up with fresh answers we appear not even to be asking the sort of questions which historians across the Channel have been doing for some thirty years'.[6] Ellis himself in *The Napoleonic Empire* (1991) started to remedy this situation by providing a useful resumé of current European research on the effect of Napoleon's activities on France and Europe. Over the last decade, however, there has been an upsurge in interest in Napoleon and his empire. While many more French works are now available in English, a considerable body of new work by British academics has appeared in print. Many of these are noted in the references and in the text.

References

1 Jean-Jaques Rousseau, *The Social Contract* (1762).
2 Michael Broers, *Europe Under Napoleon 1799–1815* (Arnold, 1996) p. 15.
3 Georges Michon (ed), *Correspondance de Maximilien et Augostine Robespierre* (Paris, 1926) p. 274.
4 Georges Lefebvre, *Napoléon* (Paris, 1935) pp. 60–6.
5 Pieter Geyl, *Napoleon: For and Against* (Penguin, 1949).
6 Geoffrey Ellis, *Napoleonic Empire* (Macmillan, 1991) p. 4.

Summary Diagram
Napoleon – an Introduction

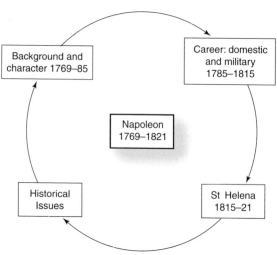

Working on Chapter 1

In this opening chapter it is more important that you grasp the main features of Napoleon's extraordinary career than to produce detailed notes. You should start to understand something about Napoleon himself – what sort of man he was and, equally importantly, the context in which he emerged so dramatically onto the French and European stage. It is quite possible that you will find that your initial views on his character will change as you progress through this book, and perhaps read others. Whatever conclusions you finally reach, whether you end up liking or loathing him, it is unlikely that you will remain indifferent to Napoleon. As a reminder of the key features of his career you could construct a diagram on the basis of the summary diagram, but in an expanded form adding material from the text of this chapter and from the key dates.

2 The *Coup* of Brumaire

POINTS TO CONSIDER

This chapter looks at the crucial events of 9–10 November 1799, known as the *coup* of Brumaire. The plot, which was hatched by two of the Directors, propelled Napoleon from a rather peripheral military role into the political limelight. You will need to understand how the circumstances of the *coup* came about, and particularly how Napoleon came to be involved in the plot. As you read this chapter for the first time, familiarise yourself with the contributory factors behind the *coup* and note why there was such a degree of opposition against the Directory. You should also note the role of others – notably that of Napoleon's brother Lucien – in helping to determine the final outcome of the plot.

KEY DATES

1795	22 August	Constitution of Year III
	1 October	Royalist Vendémiaire Uprising put down by Napoleon, who is appointed commander of the Army of the Interior
	2 November	Directory established
1796	11 March	Napoleon appointed commander in Italy
1797	September	Pro-royalist Directors and deputies purged
1798	May	Napoleon sets sail for Egypt. Deputies suspected of Jacobinism purged
1799	August	Army in Egypt abandoned by Napoleon
	October	Napoleon lands in Frejus
	9–10 November	*Coup* of Brumaire
	December	Constitution of Year VIII

1 The Political Background to the *Coup*

> **KEY ISSUES** Why did the *coup* of Brumaire take place and how did Napoleon become involved in it?

The early extremism of Revolutionary politics in France had come to an end by 1795, the year in which a new and more moderate Constitution was adopted. It aimed to secure the position of the bourgeoisie over all other groups in the political life of the nation. This was to be achieved by ensuring that political power was in the hands of the propertied classes who paid high levels of taxes.[1] The government was headed by an executive of five Directors, but with only limited powers – they had no control over legislation, for instance, for this was the prerogative of two councils. The first of these councils, the Five Hundred, could initiate legislation but not vote on it. They could then send it on for consideration to the second council, known as the Ancients (250 men all aged at least 40), who could not discuss it, but only accept or reject it. These arrangements, intended to prevent dictatorship, meant that there was no single person or body in overall control of events and led to a series of political conflicts and stalemates. The Directors could not insist that the Councils pass a particular law, neither could they veto any laws that they did pass. They could not dissolve the Councils, and the arrangements for altering the Constitution to enable them to do so were so time-consuming that it would take nine years for any change to come into legal effect.

The Directory, which lasted for four years, was the longest lasting regime of the First Republic, yet it failed to deal with the deep divisions in French society that were a legacy of the early years of the revolution. The most significant of these were religious (those for or against the Catholic Church), social (between the poor and the rich middle and upper classes) and political (republicans and royalists) Faced with a royalist uprising in the autumn of 1795 the Directory used the artillery of a young general – Napoleon Bonaparte – to deal with the rebels. It appeared that when confronted with opposition, the Directors were willing to resort to unconstitutional methods to secure majorities in the Councils. The army was used in 1797 in a *coup* to expel the newly elected royalist majority. Although Napoleon was in Italy, he sent 'the Jacobin General Augereau to Paris to defend the three ex-jacobin Directors ... from royalist elements in the legislative councils.'[2] In 1798 the Directors once again resorted to military support and annulled that year's elections because they produced a Jacobin (extreme revolutionary) majority.

By 1799 there were clear tensions within the Directory. One of the newly chosen Directors – Sieyès – planned a *coup* aimed at strengthening the executive at the expense of the more unpredictable legislative assembly. Once again it was decided to make use of the army and the plotters began looking for a popular and successful general who could organise the military support they needed to force through changes in the constitution, and who would be willing to retire gracefully from political life afterwards. Although he was not their first or even second choice, they eventually settled on Napoleon as a suitable candidate and he was recruited to the ranks of the conspirators. The result, though, was not to be what they expected – or wanted. Why was Napoleon chosen? There are a number of reasons why he was invited to join the conspiracy: his 'Jacobin' background made him a safe general as he was not a royalist; his military disasters had occurred far away in Egypt; his military record to date did not appear to suggest that he might be a general with political ambitions. 'Napoleon was a dark horse in 1799.'[3]

2 The Events of the *Coup* of Brumaire

KEY ISSUE What happened during the *coup*?

Through various sources Napoleon learned of the deteriorating political situation in France along with rumours of his wife Josephine's affairs. Napoleon decided to abandon his army in Egypt and return to France without permission before news of his recent military setbacks reached the general public. 'The circumstances in which France is placed have made it my imperative duty to return there.' Instead of being arrested for deserting his post he was greeted as a hero when he landed at Frejus on 9 October 1799. On his way to Paris he was welcomed with enthusiasm by crowds who gathered everywhere he went. The civilian population knew of his past victories in Italy and Egypt and greeted him as a hero, while the army hailed him as the leader needed to overthrow a weak government of which they were tired and that was losing touch with its Revolutionary roots. He wrote later of his triumphal journey to Paris:

> The joy was universal. It was not like the return of a citizen to his country or a general at the head of a victorious army, but like the triumph of a sovereign restored to his people. The people seemed to say, We want a leader to direct us; we now behold him and our glory will once more shine forth. I was ... resolved to possess myself of authority and restore France to her former glory. Let the deliverer give proof of his existence and the nation instinctively acknowledges and calls on him; all obstacles vanish at his approach and a great people thronging round his steps seems, exultingly, to proclaim 'This is the man!'.

Once in Paris Napoleon had a series of secret meetings with Sieyès, to discuss tactics. By early November detailed preparations were complete for a *coup* to introduce a new Constitution. A meeting of the Council of Ancients was to be called early in the morning of 9 November at which the members would be 'persuaded' that there was a plot by anarchists and foreigners to destroy the Republic. They would then agree that the government's only safety lay in moving themselves and the Council of the Five Hundred out of Paris into the suburbs, and in putting Napoleon in command of the Paris garrison of some 8000 troops and the government defence force of 1500 grenadiers. He would then be able to 'take all measures necessary for the safety of the nation's representatives', who 'in the shelter of his protecting arms may discuss peacefully the changes which the public interest renders necessary'.

The Ancients met as arranged and, after agreeing to the move from Paris, summoned Napoleon before them to swear a prepared oath of loyalty to the government. When he arrived at the council chamber, he made a speech instead, concluding with the words: 'What we want is a republic founded on true liberty, civil liberty and national representations; and we are going to have it. I swear it, in my name and in that of my comrades in arms'. Despite not being exactly what they had asked for, the Ancients accepted these words and allowed Napoleon to leave. Once outside the building he harangued his troops in much the same words as he had used to the Ancients and issued an Order of the Day expressing his belief that the army would support him 'with the energy, steadfastness and confidence' that he had always found in it before.

The following day, 10 November, after considerable delays in finding suitable furnishings for the makeshift council chambers hastily prepared in the palace of St Cloud on the outskirts of Paris, the Ancients and the Five Hundred began their deliberations just after noon. News soon reached them that all the Directors had either resigned or were under arrest, and that, without an executive, the Directory was, therefore, at an end. The way was open for the deputies to set up a new, provisional government. As the meetings of the two Councils continued without any decisions being reached, Napoleon, waiting in an outer room, became impatient. Without warning, and uninvited, he burst into the Council of the Ancients and began to speak.

Exactly what happened next is disputed. Napoleon's secretary, a hostile witness, declared that 'he made no speech to the Ancients unless a conversation held without nobility and without dignity can be called a speech. Only a few words could be heard, "brothers-in-arms", "plain-speaking of a solider" … repeating several times "That is all I have to say to you" – and he was saying nothing'. The official version of the speech, probably provided by Napoleon himself, and published the following day, was very different. Far from the 'incoherent babbling' usually attributed to him on this occasion by historians, he was represented as delivering a reasoned and statesmanlike account of his part in events to date. He denied that he was an intriguer or a political opportunist, urged the Ancients 'to act in saving liberty, saving equality', and promised that when this was done he would act as 'nothing more than the arm to support what you have established'. The report continued:

Yesterday I was staying quietly in Paris, when I was summoned by you to provide military support for the transfer to St Cloud. Now I am attacked as a new Caesar … and there is talk of a military government. But I am only acting through and for you. The Republic has abdicated – the Directors have resigned or are under police protection – the Five Hundred is at sixes and sevens. Everything depends on the Ancients …

> I am not an intriguer: you know me well enough for that: I think I have
> given sufficient pledges of my devotion to my country. If I am a traitor
> it is for each of you to be a Brutus [one of assassins of the Roman leader
> Julius Caesar]. But if anyone calls for my outlawry, then the thunderbolt
> of war shall crush him. Remember that I march hand in hand with the
> god of fortune and of war![4]

Napoleon was not an effective public speaker and the printed report
probably represents what he afterwards wished he had said, rather
than what was actually said.

Leaving the Ancients to continue their debate, Napoleon, accompanied by four grenadiers, went on to where a stormy meeting of the
Five Hundred was being held. The Jacobin majority was arguing
fiercely against a proposal that the Directory should be replaced by a
stronger executive body, when Napoleon entered the room. Again it

Napoleon and the Council of Five Hundred at St Cloud by Bouchot

is not clear exactly what happened, for there are once more a number of conflicting accounts. However, it seems that many of the Five Hundred suspected Napoleon of plotting to make himself military ruler of France under a new constitution forced through the Councils with the help of the army, for he was immediately greeted with cries of 'Outlaw the dictator'. This was a dangerous development, for if a decree of outlawry were agreed, it would mean summary execution by a firing squad.

The recently appointed president of the Five Hundred, Napoleon's brother Lucien Bonaparte, was unable to quell the disorder that immediately broke out in the chamber, or to prevent the demand that a debate be held on the proposed outlawry. Meanwhile, after being much jostled and roughly handled by some of the deputies, Napoleon was rescued by the four grenadiers who managed to escort him to safety outside in the courtyard where other soldier were waiting. Once there, pale and shaken, near fainting and incapable of action, he could only say 'I simply went to inform the deputies of the means of saving the republic, but they answered me with dagger-blows', pointing to his face that had a slight smear of blood, probably made accidentally by his own finger nails. This theme of the daggers was quickly taken up by Lucien who had hurried from the Council to join his brother:

> The president declares that the vast majority of the Council is for the moment living in terror of several representatives with stilettos ... confronting their colleagues with the most dreadful threats. These brigands are no longer representatives of the people, but of the dagger. The Five Hundred is dissolved.

Lucien then staged a dramatic scene for the benefit of the waiting troops. After denouncing 'the minority of assassins' among the deputies, he drew his sword and swore to kill his brother with it if Napoleon ever threatened the liberty of the French people. He then called on the army to follow their general and 'employ force against these disturbers'. Napoleon, now recovered from his fright, ordered the soldiers to advance against the Five Hundred. Led by an officer shouting 'Kick them all out', the men marched with fixed bayonets, and to the sound of a drum the Five Hundred were driven out of the room in less than five minutes, many of them escaping through the windows.

When the Ancients heard what had happened, they quickly agreed to the formal abolition of the Directory, the creation of a three-man executive, and the replacement of the two legislative Councils by two provisional Standing Committees of 25 members each.

By evening 'the agitators, intimidated, had dispersed and gone away' while 'others [of the Five Hundred] protected now from the [dagger] blows, came freely back to the Council room, and propositions necessary to the safety of the public were heard'. Under the chairmanship of the tireless Lucien, 'The salutary resolution which is to become the new and provisional law of the republic was discussed and prepared' by a rump of a hundred or so deputies. This 'Law of Brumaire', in addition to accepting the proposals of the Ancients, named as the three provisional consuls Sieyès, the nonentity Ducos (another former Director), and Napoleon.

> Proclamation issued by the three Consuls justifying their action, 11 November 1799
>
> The Constitution of Year III (1795) was dying. It was incapable of protecting your rights, even of protecting itself. Through repeated assaults it was losing beyond recall the respect of nations. Selfish factions were despoiling the republic. France was entering the last stage of general disorganisation. But patriots have made themselves heard. All who could harm you have been cast aside. All who can serve you, all those representatives who have remained pure have come together under the banner of liberty ... Frenchmen, the republic strengthened and restored to that rank in Europe which should never have been lost, will realise all the hopes of her citizens and will accomplish her glorious destiny. Swear with us the oath which we have taken, to be faithful to the republic, one and indivisible, founded on equality, liberty and the representative system.

The *coup* was over. The Napoleonic era was about to begin.

A contemporary British cartoon depicting
Napoleon as a crowned crocodile

3 Why was the *Coup* Successful?

> **KEY ISSUE** What factors contributed to the success of the *coup* of
> 18–19 Brumaire (9–10 November)?

A nineteenth-century French historian, de Toqueville, wrote of
Brumaire that it was 'One of the worst conceived and worst conducted *coups* imaginable, which succeeded only by virtue of the all powerful nature of its causes – the state of mind of the public and the
disposition of the army'. Was de Toqueville right in this judgement?
Were there any other factors?

The *coup* was certainly a confused affair, both in terms of its organisation and in its execution. While there was agreement between the
two central figures beforehand on their political aims, in reality this
was more apparent than real. Sieyès said afterwards that he had
intended Napoleon to destroy the Directory and then quietly withdraw, leaving the field clear for him to take control at the head of a
new executive. Napoleon later admitted that in the days before the
coup, he had promised that Sieyès' own 'wordy constitution would be
put into effect'. It seems unlikely that he made such a promise without being offered something in return; but he never admitted it. The
following are the main factors that have been used in explaining the
success of the *coup*.

i) The roles of Sieyès and Napoleon

It is possible that Sieyès wanted a *coup* that would bring about change
by peaceful means, and strengthen the executive without disturbing a
system where the bourgeoisie dominated political life. Events on 18
Brumaire went in accordance with his plans and represent the first act
of the *coup*, with Sieyès in charge. There was no public reaction and all
was quiet in the capital that night. Sieyès was confident that the
Councils would agree to his proposals in the morning but delays in
starting the meetings gave the opposition party in the Five Hundred
time to muster their objections to changes in the constitution. This,
combined with Napoleon's impatience for action, changed the whole
nature of the *coup* and marked the beginning of its second act, with
Napoleon in charge. Did Napoleon intend all along to seize control of
events? It seems probable that he did. His triumphal progress through
France on his return from Egypt, his speeches at the time, and his later
assertion that, during the weeks of discussion before the *coup*, he was
always following 'the interest of his own plans', all suggest it.

ii) The state of public opinion towards the end of 1799

Alexis de Tocqueville's wrote that 'the state of mind of the public' was a prime cause of the *coup*'s success. Opinions are divided about the state of France at the end of 1799. At one time it was fashionable to accept unquestioningly that France was socially and economically at a very low ebb towards the end of the 1790s. Roads were like 'ploughed fields', travel was dangerous because of robbers and worse, everywhere there was poverty and depravity resulting from a widespread decline in trade and industry and a breakdown of law and order. With royalist risings in the west causing civil war at home and the armies of the Second Coalition (Britain, Russia, Austria and the Ottoman Empire) threatening an invasion of France, there was defeatist talk of a Bourbon restoration and an accompanying fear that the achievements of the Revolution would be destroyed. This ultra gloomy picture is now largely discredited for it is known to have been based on reports sent in to Napoleon by his newly-appointed officials in the provinces. *The Great Survey of Year IX* and numerous pamphlets, such as *The State of France at the end of Year VIII*, constituted a determined government effort to blacken the record of the Directory and justify the *coup d'état*, to the advantage of the officials and of Napoleon himself. It is an early example of the Napoleonic propaganda machine at work.

iii) Disillusionment with the Directory

While it would be equally wrong to suggest that all was entirely well with France in 1799, it is now considered that the Directory, faced with serious problems beyond its immediate control, coped with them much better than had previously been thought. As well as making great efforts to improve the country's administrative and financial systems, it managed in a period of general economic depression to maintain and in some areas even increase French prosperity by the end of 1799. It was to be Napoleon's good fortune that a general upturn in the economy coincided with his coming to power and lasted for several years.

In other ways, too, the Directory achieved more than its successors were prepared to acknowledge. A royalist revolt was contained in southwest France and the armies of the Directory managed several, if rather minor, victories abroad against their enemies of the Second Coalition. The prospect was not entirely bleak in 1799, and most historians would now disagree with the old argument that the ease with which Napoleon seized power was due solely to the French people's 'need for a saviour' to bring order out of chaos and to restore law and order. The French historian Jean Tulard is something of an exception here.[5] He believes that Napoleon was the archetype and founding member of a long line of 'saviours, culminating in de Gaulle, and forming the chief landmarks in the history of nineteenth and twentieth century France'. In his opinion Napoleon was the 'saviour' needed by France. His mission was to preserve the security of recently acquired property (*biens nationaux*) and its owners, and to bring the Revolution to an end while maintaining its gains and stabilising its achievements. Disaster overtook him when he departed from this brief and involved France in the imperial adventure. The government was confronted by opposition from both royalists and extreme republicans. Napoleon had considerable insight into how weak the Directory was in reality and how its reliance on the army in the past could provide him with an opportunity to advance his career. The extent to which he saw himself as the saviour of France and the revolution is one of the issues you will need to consider over the following chapters.

iv) The support of the property-owning classes

What evidence is there that the property-owning classes supported Napoleon at the time of the *coup*? Property owners included large landowners and wealthy urban middle-class citizens (the bourgeoisie) who had bought up the *biens nationaux* (royalist and church lands seized by the state early in the Revolution and sold off to anyone able to pay), as well as small farmers and even a few peasants. The Revolution freed peasants from having to pay tithes to the church and feudal dues to their landlords and in some cases they had been able to buy small quantities of land. By 1795 when the Directory came to power, the constitution already embodied the ownership of private property as one of the rights guaranteed by the Revolution. Many of the new property owners, especially the bourgeoisie, feared that a Jacobin revival or a Bourbon restoration would result in a government seizure of their recent acquisitions. Either of these events might occur, they believed, under the weak government of the Directory. They welcomed, therefore, the chance of strong government offered by the return of Napoleon, who seemed likely to protect them against Jacobins and Royalists alike. In Martin Lyons' view, 'If Bonaparte was the gravedigger of political liberty, the Directory had already presented him with the corpse.'[6]

Marxist historians argue that the property-owning classes as a whole supported Napoleon because they were driven to it, whether they realised it or not, by the economic interests of the bourgeoisie. Industry and commerce needed foreign markets in order to expand. To obtain these markets would probably mean war, at least with Britain, and businessmen did not believe that the Directory would be able to win such a war. Only Napoleon, the general with the untarnished war record, could, in their view, reasonably be expected to do so.

v) Apathy

Napoleon's seizure of power does not seem initially to have aroused much public interest or enthusiasm in any class of society, property-owning or otherwise. According to Norman Hampson, 'What decided Bonaparte's victory was not so much the success of the *coup d'etat* as its favourable reception by public opinion at large. There was not much left that seemed worth fighting for'.[7] What historians have called a 'cloud of political apathy' had settled down heavily on France under the Directory, after the great upheavals of the early Revolution. It even became difficult in the late 1790s to persuade candidates to come forward for election as local officials. When the *coup* came there was little or no political reaction, probably because it appeared at first to most people to be just another of the Directory's temporary manoeuvres – a mere cosmetic substitution of consuls for directors. Not until Napoleon's policies became clear did the property-owners rally to his side and his interests become theirs.

vi) The role of the army

By 1799 the use of the army in civilian politics had become an accepted fact – the Directory had called on them successfully in 1797 and 1798 to maintain itself in power – but in 1799 the situation was different. The Directors realised too late that they had lost control of events when they put the Paris garrison of 8000 or so regular troops under Napoleon's command, especially when they failed to extract from him the very specific oath of loyalty they had at first demanded. The soldiers knew Napoleon as the General who had arranged for the Army of Italy to receive half their wages in gold and silver, not in depreciated paper money, a decision that had made him personally enormously popular, even before he won a single victory. With the glory of his Italian and Egyptian campaigns still upon him, they were well disposed to do whatever he ordered, particularly after he promised on 19 Brumaire to remedy their grievances against the government. These were mainly concerned with holes in their shoes, a shortage of tobacco and delays in payment of their wages. The *coup* could not have been carried out successfully without the intimidating presence of the army and St Cloud, nor without its help in dispersing the opposition members of the Five Hundred.

vii) The contribution of Lucien Bonaparte and support among the Ancients and the Five Hundred

There was one other small, but highly important, group of supporters of the *coup* who were extremely influential in ensuring its success. These supporters were to be found among the Ancients and the Five Hundred. Research suggests that in the weeks before the *coup* the conspirators worked hard on the deputies, and by various means, mostly financial, bought the allegiance of many of them. A great number of the Ancients were apparently given advance information on the *coup* and agreed to support it, for no difficulty of any kind was raised about moving the Councils to St Cloud, thus enabling the *coup* to take place. Even more significant was the election, immediately prior to the *coup*, of Napoleon's brother, Lucien, to be President of the Five Hundred, where he acted as a counter-balance to the Jacobin majority. His presence there proved invaluable and his role in the later stages of the *coup* was crucial to its success. Without his decisive action, his brother's bid for power would have ended prematurely, almost certainly in death, shot as an outlaw.

The whole *coup* had been a muddled affair, and had been lucky to succeed at all. 'Napoleon was the great beneficiary, but Lucien the true hero of Brumaire'.[8] Napoleon emerged as hesitant and indecisive, and with little credit. These facts, though, were speedily disguised by Napoleonic propaganda, and Lucien – after a short spell as Minister of the Interior when he made himself useful to his brother in manipulating the results of the first plebiscite – was removed from the government and sent out of the limelight into near exile as ambassador to Spain.

References

1 Dylan Rees and Duncan Townson, *France in Revolution* (Hodder and Stoughton, 2001) pp. 107–8.
2 D.G.Wright, *Napoleon and Europe* (Longman, 1984) p. 13.
3 Michael Broers, *Europe under Napoleon* (Arnold, 1996) p. 19.
4 For a longer more detailed version see Malcolm Crook, *Napoleon Comes to Power: Democracy and Dictatorship in Revolutionary France, 1795–1804* (University of Wales Press, 1998) pp. 112–13.
5 Jean Tulard, *Napoleon: The Myth of the Saviour* (Methuen, 1984).
6 Martyn Lyons, *Napoleon Bonaparte and the Legacy of the French Revolution* (Macmillan, 1994) p. 41.
7 Norman Hampson, *The French Revolution: A Concise History* (Thames and Hudson, 1975) p. 171.
8 Geoffrey Ellis, *Napoleon* (Longman, 1997) p. 32.

Summary Diagram
The *Coup* of Brumaire 1799

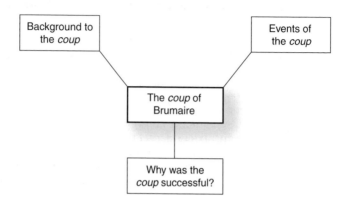

Working on Chapter 2

This chapter will have provided you with the immediate background to the *coup* of Brumaire and you should pay particular attention to three aspects of the content: (1) the situation in France in the period preceding the *coup* (*c.* 1797–99); (2) what took place during the *coup*?; and (3) what factors contributed to the success of the *coup*? You may find it useful for revision purposes to identify in a number of bullet points the main features under each aspect.

Answering structured and essay questions on Chapter 2

The recipe for success at AS and A2 is the combination of sound knowledge of the topic combined with an ability to answer directly the question that has been set by the examiner. Candidates frequently underachieve because they either fail to address the question while having a sound grasp of the topic, or understand the question but fail to deploy sufficient content to support what is required. Always read a question carefully when you first open an examination paper so that you can become fully aware of what it requires. You may find it useful to jot down a few points or a loose plan to help you compose your response. Remember to focus clearly on the question and to ensure that you deploy sufficient factual content to answer it. Examiners are very skilled in spotting candidates who deviate from the question and seek to answer a question of their own choosing.

Given the nature of this topic it is unlikely that a wide variety of questions can be set on it. The two main themes in essence are why the *coup* occurred, and was it successful.

Structured questions at AS will mainly comprise two or three parts. The first and second parts will as a rule require factual responses while the third part, which will be worth more marks, will adopt an analytical approach.

a) Why was the Directory so unpopular by 1799? (*5 marks*)
b) Explain how Napoleon came to be involved in the *coup* of Brumaire. (*10 marks*)
c) To what extent was the success of the conspirators due to popular support? (*15 marks*)

When starting your answer, remember that the marks in brackets are an indication of the proportion of the exam time you should spend on each part. In part **a** you should simply note some of the factors that accounted for the Directory's unpopularity – such as its use of force to suppress risings and its failure to heal the divisions within French society. Do not spend too much time on this question. Part **b** will require you to explain why Napoleon was invited to join the conspiracy – why Sieyès considered him to be useful; Napoleon's own personal ambition which led him to abandon his army in Egypt in order to position himself if any opportunity arose. Spend at least half the allotted time on part **c**. You are provided with one factor which you will need to evaluate along with others which you will need to introduce. These should include, among others, the role of the army, general apathy and the role of Lucien Bonaparte.

The following are some essay questions linked to this topic.

1 Can Napoleon's rise to power be attributed merely to his control of the army?
2 'Napoleon's rise to power was solely due to his control of the army.' Discuss.

It is very important that you answer the question, which has been set, and that you do not adopt a narrative approach in your answer. Essay questions require analysis and evaluation and the factual content should be deployed when appropriate in support of an argument. In Question 1 you will need to consider the way in which Napoleon's position as one of the highest profile generals of the First Republic contributed to his rise to power. While his control of the army was an important factor, the domestic issues facing the Directory and the general lack of support for the regime will also need to be examined in a balanced way. Question 2 is in some ways a variation of Question 1 although it provides you with a key word, 'solely', upon which to hang your response. There were clearly other factors that explain his rise to power in addition to his 'control of the army', which in any case could be questioned as he was not the first choice of the other conspirators.

Source-based questions on Chapter 2

I   Napoleon and the *coup* of Brumaire

Read carefully the three extracts by Napoleon on pages 12, 13 and 16 and answer the following questions:

a) Explain briefly the meaning of (i) the Directors, (ii) the Ancients, and (iii) the Five Hundred. (*6 marks*)

b) What sort of reception, according to Napoleon, did he receive from his fellow citizens? (*5 marks*)

c) What arguments does Napoleon use to justify his actions in helping to overthrow the Directory? (*10 marks*)

d) Using the sources and your own knowledge, explain why the *coup* of Brumaire occurred? (*20 marks*)

3 Napoleon and France: Politics and Power

POINTS TO CONSIDER

Following the seizure of power in 1799, Napoleon embarked on a far-reaching programme of domestic reforms. His approach to governing France and the policies he introduced have been the subject of debate over whether he forms a continuous link with the revolution or, rather, reverts in a number of significant ways to the *ancien régime*. The focus of this chapter is on how Napoleon consolidated his power, and the reform programme that he initiated. As you read the chapter for the first time, try to note carefully the methods he employed to preserve his authority. You should ask yourself, which groups did he attempt to cultivate to ensure that he remained in power? The chapter also tries to assess the nature of the regime over which Napoleon ruled. A number of views are provided and you should consider whether they provide a valid assessment of Napoleon's policies.

KEY DATES

1799	December	Constitution of Year VIII introduced
1800	January	New Constitution approved by plebiscite
	February	Creation of Bank of France
1801	15 July	Concordat with Pope
1802	1 May	Beginning of educational reorganisation with creation of *lycées*
	19 May	Legion of Honour established
	2 August	Plebiscite confirms Napoleon *Consul for life*
	16 August	Constitution of Year X
1803	April	Introduction of workman's *livret*
1804	20 March	Kidnapping and execution of Duke of Enghien
	21 March	Introduction of the Civil Code
	18 May	Senate proclaims Napoleon Emperor of the French
		Constitution of Year XII approved by plebiscite
	2 December	Coronation at Notre Dame
1808	17 March	Imperial University established

1 Establishing Power

> **KEY ISSUES** What were the main features of the new constitution?
> To what extent were they based on representative government?

The successful conclusion of the *coup* was only the beginning for
Napoleon. He had gained political power, but needed to consolidate
it if he were to make himself undisputed ruler of France. He began
with the constitution.

a) The Constitution

Late in the evening of 19 Brumaire year VIII (10 November 1799) the
three newly-elected provisional consuls (Napoleon, Sieyès and Ducos)
swore an oath of allegiance to the Republic. At the same time
Napoleon issued his first Proclamation:

> On my return to France I found that the Constitution was half
> destroyed and no longer capable of maintaining our liberty ... The
> Council of Ancients called on me – I answered the appeal ... I offered
> myself to the Five Hundred, my head uncovered, alone, unarmed ...
> twenty assassins rushed upon me, aiming at my breast ...

Within a few hours of the *coup* there were expressions of anxiety
among the *philosophes* (liberal intellectuals interested in the general
philosophy of government and society) particularly when it became
known that under the Law of Brumaire the two legislative councils
had been adjourned. On 20 Brumaire Benjamin Constant warned
Sieyès that

> This step appears disastrous to me in that it destroys the only barrier
> against a man with whom you associated yesterday but who is threat-
> ening the republic. His proclamations, in which he speaks only of him-
> self and says that his return has given rise to the hope that he will end
> France's troubles, have convinced me more than ever that in everything
> he does he sees only his own advancement.

In the Luxembourg Palace in Paris the consuls set to work on the
new constitution, bypassing the two Standing Committees that were
supposed to draw up the draft plans. In a series of long and often
heated discussions Sieyès' proposed that Napoleon should occupy the
role of a figurehead in the new constitution. Napoleon refused to
countenance the idea. There must, he argued, be a *First Consul* as
head of state with complete control, in peace and in war, at home and
abroad; and *he* must be that consul. The roles of the second and third
consuls also caused argument. Sieyès wanted them each to have *voix
deliberative* (the right to one of three equal votes). Napoleon, however,
insisted they should have only *voix consultative* (the right merely to

express an opinion). In all matters his decision would be final. Faced with Napoleon's domineering personality, Sieyès was eventually forced into the humiliating position of having to make the official nomination of Napoleon as *First Consul*. All three consuls would serve initially for ten years.

The negotiations had taken about six weeks to complete. In this time the government of France had been transformed from one where political responsibility was spread as widely as possible to one where it was centralised in the hands of a single man – a dictator. Sieyès was compensated for the ruin of his plans and the loss of his hoped for consulship by being given the presidency of the Senate and a large estate in the country. 'Gentlemen, you have got yourselves a master', he is reported to have said of Napoleon at the end of the negotiations, 'a man who knows everything, wants everything, and can do everything'.

In a proclamation Napoleon explained to the French people his reasons for seizing power:

> To make the Republic loved by its own citizens, respected abroad and feared by its enemies – such are the duties we have assumed in accepting the *First Consulship*

and he added reassuringly that the new constitution was

> based upon the true principles of representative government and on the sacred rights of property, equality and liberty. The powers it sets up will be strong and lasting.

But was this in fact the case? Was the constitution based on representative government? The electoral system adopted at the beginning of the consulate was Sieyès' invention and certainly provided for 'universal suffrage', unlike the property-based vote of the 1795 constitution. But this suffrage was so indirect as to be of little significance in relation to the idea of popular sovereignty (that is, the idea that the people should exercise control over their government, usually by directly electing a representative assembly). There were, it is estimated, about 6 million 'Frenchmen of the age of 21 with a year's domicile' named as voters on the commune registers in 1799. Women were not given any role in the new political system. These 6 million men chose 10% of their number to form a communal list (from whom local officials would be drawn), and that was the end of the direct vote. These 600,000 in turn chose 10% of their number to form a departmental list, and these finally chose 6000 of themselves to go on to a national list of 'persons fit for public service'. From this national list of 'notables' the Senate chose the members of the two legislative bodies – the Tribunate of 100 members aged 25 or more who could discuss legislation but could not vote on it, and a Legislature of 300 members aged 30 or more who could vote on legislation by secret ballot but could not discuss it. The Senate (some 60 distinguished men aged 40 or more, and holding office for life) was itself nominated by the *First Consul*, who also presided over the Council of state of 30 to 40 men, who were chosen by him. The Council nominated all major central and local government officials, and initiated all legislation.

The references to a constitution based on representative government were merely words. Democratic involvement in the elections was minimal. While there was the appearance of adult male suffrage, there were no *elections*, only *presentations* of candidates suitable for appointment as deputies, and the choice of candidates was restricted to notables – men of wealth, usually landowners or existing government officials. It is possible to see the Consulate as 'a compromise between the victories of the Revolution and the institutions of the old monarchy minus King and nobility'.[1]

Power was firmly in the hands of one man (the *First Consul*), who stood alone at the top of the political pyramid. He controlled government appointments, made and unmade ministers whom he closely supervised and to whom he allowed no freedom of action, initiated all legislation through the Council of State or the Senate, declared war and made peace. The Senate, which had been intended by Sieyès to act as a brake on the executive, became under Napoleon's leadership an instrument of his personal power. As Albert Soboul pointed out: 'The authoritarian regime that the Brumairians had wanted to install switched dramatically to favour the increase of Bonaparte's personal power. In a startling metamorphosis, the Republic of Notables became a military dictatorship.'[2] The Senate was supposed to be the guardian of the existing constitution, but was also able to amend it by a legal procedure known as *senatus-consultum*. It was this procedure that Napoleon used extensively from January 1801 onwards in order to thwart the wishes of the Tribunate and the Legislature. Appointed for life, with a substantial salary and suitably rewarded with gifts of land and money, the Senators enjoyed considerable prestige. Membership of the Senate increased from the original 80 to about 140 by 1814, most of the extra members being Napoleon's direct nominees or 'grand dignatories' of the Empire, used to pack the Senate. As a result it developed into a largely consultative body anxious to please its benefactor and president, Napoleon.

Under the Law of Brumaire the new constitution, in order to become legal, had to be 'submitted to the acceptance of the French people'. In February 1800 a plebiscite was held and the electors were given a month in which to vote in their communes for or against the constitution. The official results showed 3,011,007 voting in favour with 1562 against. This was not quite as overwhelming a display of public approval as the figures suggest. Voting took place at different times in different places, and the ballot was not a secret one. Voters simply wrote 'yes' or 'no' against their names on an open list. Not surprisingly, malpractice and intimidation affected the results in some areas. The government, made aware of the

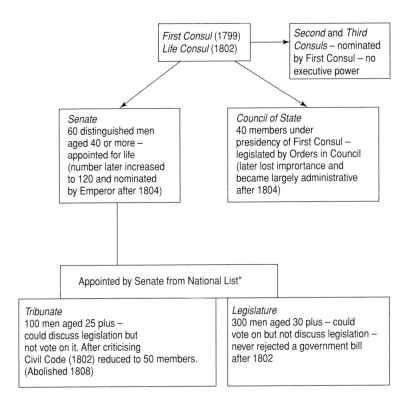

First Consul (1799)
Life Consul (1802)

Second and Third Consuls – nominated by First Consul – no executive power

Senate
60 distinguished men aged 40 or more – appointed for life (number later increased to 120 and nominated by Emperor after 1804)

Council of State
40 members under presidency of First Consul – legislated by Orders in Council (later lost imprortance and became largely administrative after 1804)

Appointed by Senate from National List*

Tribunate
100 men aged 25 plus – could discuss legislation but not vote on it. After criticising Civil Code (1802) reduced to 50 members. (Abolished 1808)

Legislature
300 men aged 30 plus – could vote on but not discuss legislation – never rejected a government bill after 1802

*Drawing up the lists took so long that the full scheme was never put into operation. It was amended in 1802 into an allegedly more democratic form of 'colleges' or Boards chosen by the Commune 'voters' from among the richest men in each department.

National List* made up of 6000 men 'fit for public service' – chosen by First Consul from this list:- prefects of departments, sub-perfects, maires, and other local officials and council members

60,000 members in 98 departments formed Departmental List – chose 10% of themselves as National List

600,000 members of Communal List chose 10% of themselves for Departmental List

†This figure of 6 million 'voters' is the usually accepted one, but it may have been as high as 8 million

† 6,000,000 'voters' in 40,000 communes chose 10% of themselves to form Communal List from which JPs were chosen

Government under the Consulate 1799–1804

problem of possible later victimisation, promised to burn all lists when the votes had been counted. However, this promise was not kept and in many parts of France the lists are still available for study.

As the constitution had already been put (illegally) into operation, there was very little point in voting 'no', especially as many people feared that to do so might lead to trouble afterwards. Although a favourable vote would merely ratify what had occurred it was important to the government's credibility that the constitution should seem to be as widely accepted as possible. There is little doubt that before the voting figures were published they were adjusted by Lucien as Minister of the Interior in order to ensure a large majority for the government. He almost doubled the total number of 'yes' votes, rounding up the figures by about 900,000 and then adding in another 500,000 to represent the unanimously favourable votes it was alleged that the army would have cast if they had been included in the plebiscite. The real 'yes' vote was, therefore, probably only about 1,500,000. In addition, recent research has suggested that the number of those eligible to vote in the communes was probably much nearer 8,000,000 than the figure of 6,000,000 previously accepted by historians. The 'yes' votes therefore represented not over 50% of the electorate, as once appeared, but only something under 20%. Even if it were argued that the large number of abstentions ought to be considered as 'not opposed' to the new régime, it does not appear that public opinion *was* sufficiently well inclined towards Napoleon and the new constitution at the beginning of 1800 to justify him regarding he result as a vote of confidence. The results of the plebiscite would appear to indicate public apathy rather than anything else.

It took a long time to draw up the massive communal, departmental and national lists, and the whole 'electoral' system proved extremely cumbersome when it was eventually put into operation in 1801. This was so much so that Napoleon abolished the system the following year even before all the lists were complete. He introduced a new arrangement that lasted until the end of the Empire and which reduced still further the element of popular choice. It was intended to produce groups of people who would act as intermediaries between government and people. All adult males met to elect life members to departmental 'colleges', or boards. However, the electors had only a limited choice of candidates, for these life members had to

Table 1 Plebicites held during the Consulate and Empire: 1800–15

Year	Purpose of Plebiscite	Voting Yes	Voting No.
1800	Constitution of Year VIII	1,550,000	1562
1802	Plebiscite on Life Consulate	3,653,000	8272
1804	Plebiscite on Empire	3,572,329	2569
1815	Plebiscite on *Acte Additionnel*	1,552,942	5740

be selected from a list of the 600 most heavily taxed and therefore the richest men in the department. Every five years the colleges produced lists of candidates for election to vacancies on the legislative bodies, but their main function was to provide readily available groups of wealthy property owners (notables) for Napoleon to court with offers of central or local government posts or other benefits. In return for these favours he expected them to bring their wealth and influence to bear on behalf of the régime. It was an arrangement by which Napoleon not only rewarded the property-owning classes for past support but also secured their loyalty for the future. It was to remain a favourite political manoeuvre until his final defeat.

How did the new Bonapartist Constitution of Year VIII relate to the revolutionary period? In a number of ways it 'established a framework for cementing in place the main social changes brought about by the French Revolution'.[3] Among the most important of these changes was the vast transfer of land that had taken place largely at the expense of the Catholic Church, but also from the nobility. It was necessary to bind the beneficiaries of these transfers to the new regime. This was achieved by creating a political system which favoured the well off propertied classes. Power in the new regime was far more centralised than it had been under the Directory, in a way it was a reversion back to the Jacobin phase of the Revolution (1793–4) when France was governed by a dictatorship. By cultivating the support of notables Napoleon was seeking to incorporate and consolidate the new élite of talent and property that had emerged since 1789.

b) The Hereditary Principle

Napoleon only narrowly escaped assassination in December 1800, making the Senate anxiously aware of the fragile nature of a régime dependent for its continuation upon one man. Partly because of this, and partly as a demonstration of gratitude to the *First Consul* for his achievements at home and abroad, it was decided to offer him the Consulship for life, with the right to nominate his successor. It was the first step towards the re-introduction of hereditary rule. Napoleon accepted 'if the will of the people demands it', and so another plebiscite was held. The result was similar to that of 1799 (an alleged 3,600,000 in favour of making Napoleon *Life Consul* and 8374 against). It is interesting to note that 40% of the 'no' votes came from the army, which had been allowed to take part in the plebiscite this time. While there is no evidence that the central government tampered directly with the figures, it is known that local officials often sent in results which they thought would be pleasing to their superiors, sometimes even recording a unanimous 'yes' vote when, in fact, no poll at all had been held.

In his speech of thanks to the senate for his appointment to the *Life Consulship*, Napoleon remarked that much still remained to be done to strengthen the constitution. One thing that was done almost immediately was to increase Napoleon's personal power through his control of an enlarged Senate, which became responsible for 'everything not provided for by the constitution, and necessary to its working'. This arrangement was greatly to the detriment of the representative bodies, the Tribunate and the Legislature. They lost much of their importance, and met more and more infrequently. The Tribunate was severely purged in 1802 for daring to criticise the Civil Code (see page 40), and with a much reduced membership became little more than a rubber stamp for the remainder of its existence, while the Legislature's credibility was reduced by being 'packed' by Napoleon with 'safe' men who would not oppose his wishes.

By 1803 Napoleon was riding in splendour around Paris and holding court in royal style. State ceremonies multiplied, etiquette was formalised, official dress became more elaborate. The Legion of Honour (see page 35) had been introduced the previous year and there were hints that a nobility was to be re-established, the rumours fired by Napoleon's permission for a large number of *emigrés* to return to France. In 1804 a series of disasters, royalist plots and counter-plots culminated in the affair of the Duc d'Enghien, a member of the Bourbon royal family alleged to be involved in a plot to supplant Napoleon by murdering him and taking over the government. The Duke was kidnapped by Napoleon's orders while on neutral territory, tried and, on very inadequate evidence, found guilty of conspiracy. He was quickly executed in what amounted to judicial murder, justified by Napoleon on the grounds that he was entitled by the Corsican laws of vendetta to kill an enemy who threatened his personal safety:

> The great number of plots which are woven against my life inspire no fear in me. But I cannot deny a deep feeling of distress when I consider the situation in which the great people would have found itself today had the recent attempt [at assassination] succeeded.

In the wake of these events Napoleon began to prepare the people for his next step. Others apart from Napoleon were considering what would happen to France if he should be murdered. The property-owners took seriously the Bourbon pretender's recent threat to return all 'stolen properties' to their 'rightful owners' as soon as he regained the throne, and most were convinced that only Napoleon stood between them and the loss of all they had gained by the Revolution. There was widespread talk of making the *Consulship* hereditary in the Bonaparte family, in the hope of providing for a smooth succession and the survival of the constitution should Napoleon meet an untimely death. Then, in May 1804, a formal motion was approved by the Senate that 'Napoleon Bonaparte at present *First Consul* be declared Emperor of the French, and that the imperial dignity be declared hereditary in his family'.

A third plebiscite was held in November 1804 asking the people whether they agreed that 'the hereditary and imperial dignity should descend through the direct natural, legitimate and adoptive heirs of Napoleon Bonaparte and the direct natural and legitimate heirs of Joseph Bonaparte and of Louis Bonaparte' (Lucien and Jérôme were pointedly excluded by Napoleon from the succession because he considered their wives to be unsuitable). The wording of the plebiscite was chosen to overcome the difficulty that Napoleon and his wife Josephine had no children, but to allow for a successor to come from within the Bonaparte family – an important point for a Corsican. The plebiscite achieved the desired result (3,572,329 'yes' and 2569 'no' votes). Remembering the adverse army vote two years earlier, the government took no chances this time and did not actually poll the soldiers. They simply added in about half a million 'yes' votes on their behalf.

At a sumptuous ceremony in the cathedral of Notre Dame in Paris held in the presence of the Pope, Napoleon, as previously arranged, took the imperial crown and placed it on his own head, before himself crowning Josephine as Empress. In his coronation oath Napoleon swore:

> to uphold the integrity of the Republic's territory, to respect and impose the laws of the Concordat and the laws of equal rights, political and civil liberties, the irrevocability of the sale of national property, to raise no duty and establish no tax except through the law, to uphold the institution of the Legion of Honour, and to rule only in the interests of the happiness and glory of the French people.

During the next two or three years the Tribunate and the Legislature were hardly consulted at all. The Tribunate was finally abolished in 1808 and, although the Legislature survived, it was only able to do so by maintaining its subservient attitude to Napoleon's demands. Government was increasingly conducted through the Senate and the Council of State, both of which were firmly under Napoleon's personal control. In theory the senate acquired important new powers in 1804 with the formation of two standing committees, one concerned with preserving individual liberty and the other with safeguarding freedom of the press. From the outset, in fact, these committees were rendered impotent by Napoleon. Neither was allowed any real opportunity to consider complaints, and only a handful of cases were dealt with in ten years. The committee on freedom of the press was further handicapped by being debarred from considering anything connected with the publication of newspapers or periodicals!

Only one thing more was needed to establish the Napoleonic dynasty beyond question – the production of a legitimate son and heir. Napoleon went about it in his usual determined way. Despite his continued fondness for her, Josephine, now past child-bearing age, would have to be divorced, and a new wife selected; but first the Church had to be persuaded that Josephine should be set aside. This was not easy, for although their original marriage had been a civil one, the Church had insisted on a second, Catholic ceremony as a necessary preliminary to the coronation in 1804. Eventually, on the grounds of alleged irregularities in the conduct of the religious marriage, the Church agreed unwillingly to an annulment, leaving Napoleon free to remarry. A list of 18 eligible princesses was drawn up for him. In 1810, at the age of 40, he married the young Marie-Louise of Austria, a niece of Marie-Antoinette (Louis XVI's wife who had been executed during the Revolution). In the following year the hoped-for son, Napoleon, King of Rome, was born. The succession seemed assured, the dynasty secure. 'I am at the summit of my happiness' Napoleon is reported to have said.

2 Maintaining Power

> **KEY ISSUE** What methods did Napoleon use to try to maintain power?

One of the first needs of the new government was money – there were only a few thousand francs in the Treasury in November 1799. In January 1800 the Bank of France was founded. At first it was a private venture, but it came under state control in 1806 and did much to establish the creditworthiness of the state. Also in 1800 the Treasury itself was reorganised to oversee the receipt, transfer and payment of state funds, and to audit state finances. A new and much more complete tax register was introduced for most of the country and the collection of direct taxes on land, personal income, and industrial profits was greatly improved through the development of a centralised hierarchy of tax-collectors working under the control of the Ministry of Finances in Paris. With the additional revenue from indirect taxes on consumer goods (the *droits réunis*) and from customs and other duties, by 1802 the state could meet its obligations on salaries and pensions, and government bonds rose in value. Napoleon had a hatred of paper money – the *assignats* of the early 1790s had been a disaster, its value declining to a point where it had became virtually worthless – and in 1803 he introduced a new metal coinage based primarily on a silver franc to replace earlier debased issues and to provide France with a strong and stable currency. As the result of these financial measures the country was solvent. Not until military expenditure began to outstrip available income in the years after 1806 did the financial situation deteriorate into annual deficit. Before that happened, however, Napoleon had acquired a stranglehold on power by pursuing a policy of uniformity and centralisation that brought all aspects of French life under his personal control.

a) Patronage and Bribery

Napoleon continued to favour property-owners and would-be property-owners throughout his time in power. He used gifts of money, land, titles, honours and government appointments to build up a strong body of personal support for himself, bind men to his service and ensure loyalty to his régime, particularly among the military. In 1802 he set up the Legion of Honour. This was divided into 15 cohorts (groups) each comprising 350 legionaries, 30 officers, 20 commandants and seven grand officers. Recipients received a distinctive decoration and a small annual award: 250 francs a year, rising to 5000 francs for grand officers.[4] In the 12 years following its establishment, 38,000 awards (only 4000 of which went to civilians) were made. Between 1804 and 1808, new titles were created for the officials of the new imperial court. These ranged from 'grand dignatories' such as the arch-chancellor, through 'grand officers', down to lesser dignatories such as the prefects of the palace. Some of these titles brought with them large estates, and although these at first went only to members of the Bonaparte family, they were soon being bestowed on court officials and statesmen, as well as on the 18 outstanding generals who were created Marshals of France. The estates awarded to these generals were mostly in Poland, Germany and Italy. It was therefore probable that Napoleon's intention was to appeal to these men's self-interest to his own advantage. They knew that the only way of retaining their property was to remain loyal to Napoleon in the hope of maintaining the Empire's frontiers.

In 1808 Napoleon went further and began the creation of a whole new imperial nobility. All 'grand dignatories' became princes, archbishops became counts, mayors of large towns became barons, and members of the Legion of Honour were allowed to call themselves Chevaliers. These titles were awarded directly by the Emperor for state service, usually of a military kind. If the recipient possessed a large enough annual income – 200,000 francs in the case of a duke for instance – the titles could be made hereditary. Where worthy candidates for ennoblement had insufficient personal fortunes to support a title they were provided, like the generals, with estates in far-off parts of the Empire from which to raise the necessary revenue. In all, about 3500 titles were granted between 1808 and 1814. One area in which civilians benefited was in the allocation of *senatoreries*. These were grants of large country estates to members of the Senate, together with a palatial residence and an annual income of 25,000 francs to support it. Included in the grant was appointment as *préfet* (prefect) not just of the usual *département* but of a whole region. Lesser individuals also benefited from Napoleon's personal gifts. For instance, more than 5000 presents of enough money to buy a house in Paris and to live there in comfort were made to army officers, government officials and minor members of the new nobility.

However, Napoleon seems to have realised from the beginning that bribery as a means of control was unreliable, and was not in itself enough to maintain popular support even among the recipients. Therefore, compulsion, intimidation and indoctrination all became part of the Napoleonic system of government.

b) Reforms and Restrictions

The restriction of individual liberty of thought, word and deed was an important element in Napoleon's autocratic government. By numerous measures, some more subtle than others, he built up over the years a system of supervision and control worthy of a modern dictator.

i) Agents of control – police and prefects

In European usage the word 'police' covers the people entrusted with the administration and operation of the entire system of rules and regulations for the maintenance of public order and state security. Napoleon's police system was an important part of his centralised administration.

A number of changes were made to the judiciary. Judges, apart from local justices of the peace, instead of being elected as under the Directory, were appointed by the government for life and were kept subservient and loyal by a combination of close supervision and a system of 'purges'. A whole new hierarchy of judicial tribunals was set up. The Criminal, Commercial and Penal Codes were updated in a similar way to the Civil Code. The Criminal and Penal Codes were essentially concerned with punishment – perpetual hard labour, loss of the right hand and branding were among the penalties laid down. Special new courts proliferated – there were military courts and tribunals for political offenders presided over by 'magistrates for public security'. In 1810 a system of arbitrary imprisonment without trial (similar to the *lettres de cachet* used in pre-revolutionary France) was reintroduced, although it was never extensively used, a form of house arrest being more usual. A number of extra prisons were built and, although figures are difficult to come by, it is estimated that in 1814 they were occupied by about 16,000 ordinary convicts (more than three times as many as in 1800).

The general police, operating under the control of the Minister of Police (Joseph Fouché, for much of the Napoleonic era) had very wide ranging powers. In Paris they were employed to monitor the state of public opinion in the city and to report daily on variations in food prices.

Today everyone is very concerned about Spain and what is going on there. As usual it is all exaggerated. The Ministry of Police has taken measures to quash false rumours. People are no longer complaining about the high price of coffee and sugar; many people go without them.

JOSEPH FOUCHÉ
DUKE OF OTRANTE
(1758–1820)

Joseph Fouché was one of the most ruthless and feared men of the revolutionary and Napoleonic period and also one of its greatest survivors – a remarkable achievement given his passion for conspiracy and plotting against his superiors.

Born in 1758 near Nantes, Fouché considered becoming a priest but was never ordained. During the early period of the revolution he was a Jacobin and was chosen President of the Nantes Jacobin club. In September 1792 he was elected to the Convention, and voted for the execution of Louis XVI. As a loyal Jacobin, Fouché was sent on missions to the provinces to supervise government forces fighting the rebels. His advice to republicans on how to deal with the uncommitted; '... run them through with the republican weapon the bayonet'. When news reached Lyon that Toulon had been recaptured Fouché's response was: 'There is only one way for us to celebrate the victory; this evening we are sending 213 rebels to face the cannon blast' (a particularly brutal way of administering mass executions). While on missions, Fouché actively supported the policy of 'dechrisianisation': church property – gold and silver – was to be systematically plundered and sent back to Paris, while cemeteries were to be stripped of religious emblems and their gates inscribed with the words 'Death is an eternal Slumber'.

During the Directory he was appointed minister of police in July 1799 and supported the *coup* of Brumaire. Napoleon invited him to organise his secret police. In 1802 his ministry was closed because he attempted to prevent the Senate making Napoleon Consul for life. Differences with Napoleon were patched up after he supported the proclamation of the Empire, and he was reinstated as minister of police. Napoleon, believing that Fouché was loyal, rewarded him by making him Duke of Ortante and also appointing him minister of the interior. The trust was misplaced. Fouché, doubting that France could win a prolonged war, began secret negotiations with Royalists and the British. Napoleon dismissed him in October 1809, following rumours of his activities.

For the next three years Fouché lived in semi-enforced retirement at Aix-en-Provence. Napoleon still considered him a threat and, in order to get him out of France, appointed him governor of the Illyrian Provinces in 1812. When Austria occupied these, he was sent on a mission to Naples where he plotted against Napoleon, with the King, Joachim Murat. After Napoleon's fall in 1814, Fouché switched allegiance to the restored monarchy, before backing Napoleon during the Hundred Day campaign. After Waterloo he advised Napoleon to abdicate and was himself elected president of a provisional government. Louis XVIII made him, once again, minister of police. By now, however, Fouché's past was starting to catch up with him and extreme royalists denounced him as a regicide in 1816. His remaining years were spent in permanent exile.

In their capacity as trained spies they acted in connection with the imposition of censorship, the surveillance of possible subversives, the search for army deserters and the organisation of raids on areas believed to be sheltering draft dodgers or enemy agents. They were assisted in their more mundane police duties such as the maintenance of law and order by the well-organised body of gendarmes, of whom there were about 18,000 stationed throughout France in 1810. Reports were submitted to Napoleon daily by Fouché on the work of his department, but Napoleon also had other sources of information. He had a spy network of his own, operating independently of Fouché, a secret police whose activities caused considerable public anxiety. Letters were opened, reports made, reputations destroyed, and careers blighted as the result of information collected for Napoleon by these men – but not only by them. A wide variety of provincial officials were expected to act as spies in the course of their work, and to relay their findings back to Paris.

The prefects (*préfets*) of *départements* or sub-prefects (*sous-préfets*) of the *arrondissements* making up each department acted as agents of the central government and were directly appointed by Napoleon. So too were the members of their advisory councils, and the mayors (*maires*) of the larger communes. The other mayors and all the municipal councils were nominated by the prefect. The result was a highly centralised bureaucracy for the collection of taxes, the enforcement of conscription, the dissemination of propaganda, and the obtaining of information, operating through a body of well-trained and loyal administrators. Richard Cobb described the whole structure as 'bureaucratic repression'.[5] The prefects, in particular, were expected to monitor public opinion in their areas and to report on any suspicious political activity. A system of house arrest was available through the prefects for anyone who did not warrant imprisonment but who was considered a danger to state security

LUCIEN BONAPARTE'S EXPLANATION TO THE PREFECTS OF THEIR MISSION, 1800

This post demands of you a wide range of duties, but it offers you great rewards in the future ... Your first task is to destroy irrevocably in your department, the influence of those events which for too long have dominated our minds. Do your utmost to bring hatred and passion to an end ... In your public decisions, be always the first magistrate of your department, never a man of the revolution. Do not tolerate any public reference to the labels which still cling to the diverse political parties of the revolution; merely consign them to the most deplorable chapter in the history of human folly ... apply yourself immediately to the conscription draft ... I give special priority to the collection of taxes: their prompt payment is now a sacred duty. Agriculture, trade, the industries and professions must resume their honoured status. Respect and honour our farmers ... Protect our trade ... Visit our manufacturers: bestow your highest compliments on those distinguished citizens engaged in them ... Encourage the new generations; fix your attention on public education, and the formation of Men, Citizens and Frenchmen.

Not very different were the obligations laid on senators when proceeding to their *senatoreries*. Napoleon wrote to them at length:

Your most important duty will be to supply Us with trustworthy and positive information on any point which may interest the government, and to this end, you will send Us a direct report, once a week ... You will realise that complete secrecy must be observed as this is a confidential mission ... You will draw up detailed returns of all information about these persons [public officials, the clergy, teachers, men of importance, farmers, industrialists, criminals] basing your information upon facts and send the reports in to Us. You will observe the condition of the roads ... and investigate the state of public opinion on (i) the government (ii) religion (iii) conscription (iv) direct and indirect taxation ...

With such well-organised surveillance it is not surprising that the régime met with little serious political opposition, especially as its potential leaders, notables, intellectuals and members of the bourgeoise, were increasingly tempted into allying themselves with the government in the hope of rewards. The only means of opposition open to the ordinary people were resisting conscription, deserting once enlisted (despite the ferocious penalties it incurred) or joining one of the bands of brigands that operated on a grand scale in much of the French countryside. Conscription had always been unpopular ever since it was introduced in 1793, but recent research shows that, until the massive levies of 1813, resistance to it was much less under Napoleon than it had been under the Directory. Over 90% of the expected levies were raised without difficulty in the years before 1808. It may have been partly due to better administration, but while Napoleon was winning victories and casualties were low, resistance to conscription was not a serious problem. Only when the military tide turned against him (from 1812) and the casualties mounted did it become so.

i) The Civil Code

The basis of the legal system, the Civil Code of 1804, later known as the *Code Napoléon*, was founded on the work of successive Revolutionary governments that had tried to organise some sort of acceptable nationwide legal system out of the conflicting customary laws of the north and the Roman law of the south. The early 1790s had seen a bias towards a system based on the liberal customary law with its acceptance of the equality of persons, civil marriage, divorce and the equal division of property between heirs; but from 1795 there had been a reaction in favour of the more authoritarian Roman law (a heritage from the days of the Roman Empire) that emphasised male authority and the father's rights. The Civil Code was strongly influenced by the precepts of Roman law – they accorded well with Napoleon's own views on society and the inferior status of women – and although it was the work of professional lawyers, Napoleon himself took a very active interest in its formulation, presiding personally over nearly half the sessions of the Senate that were devoted to its discussion.

The Code has been praised as the 'Most impressive of all the legislative measures carried out by the *First Consul*.[6] Yet while it is an important reform for its clear and understandable presentation of the law, the Code itself was in many ways illiberal and restrictive in outlook, even by the standards of the day. Individual male rights to ownership of property were maintained and the civil rights of Frenchmen were assured, but married women fared badly under its double standards. A man had total authority over his wife and family – he could send an adulterous wife or defiant child to prison – and divorce, although permitted in theory, was made very difficult and expensive to obtain. There was a lack of liberty too in the treatment of black people and workers. Slavery was reintroduced in the French colonies 'in accordance with the laws current in 1789', and workmen were made subject to close police supervision through use of the *livret*, a combined work-permit and employment record, without which it was impossible legally to obtain a job. The Code did, however, give legal sanction to some of the important developments of the 1790s – confirming the abolition of feudalism, and giving fixed legal title to those who had earlier purchased confiscated church, crown and emigré property (the *biens nationaux*). It also followed the Revolutionary principle of *partage*, that is, equal division of estates among male heirs instead of primogeniture (whereby the eldest son inherited everything).

iii) Censorship and Propaganda

The press was expected to act as the unquestioning mouthpiece of the government and to be the purveyor of official propaganda. Napoleon wrote

> The newspapers are always ready to seize on anything which might undermine public tranquility ... Newspapers ... announce and prepare revolutions and in the end make them indispensable. With a smaller number of newspapers it is easier to supervise them and to direct them more firmly towards the strengthening of the constitutional régime ... I will never allow the newspapers to say or do anything against my interest.

In January 1800 he arbitrarily reduced the number of political journals published in Paris from 73 to 13 and forbade the production of any new ones. By the end of the year only nine remained. These survivors were kept short of reliable news and were forbidden to discuss controversial subjects. Their editors were forced to rely for news on the military bulletins or longer political articles published in *Le Moniteur*, the official government journal. These were written by Napoleon himself or by his ministers, and 'to lie like a bulletin' soon became a common saying. In 1809 censors were appointed to each newspaper and a year later provincial papers were reduced to one per department. In 1811 all except four of the Parisian papers were suppressed and those that remained were made subject to police supervision.

It was not only newspapers that were censored. Up to 1810 reports on all books, plays, lectures and posters that appeared in Paris were sent, often daily, to Napoleon, and publishers were required to forward two copies of every book, prior to publication, to police headquarters. In 1810 a regular system of censors was set up, more than half the printing presses in Paris were shut down, and publishers were forced to take out a licence and to swear an oath of loyalty to the government. Booksellers were strictly controlled and severely punished, even with death, if found to be selling material considered subversive. Authors were harassed and sometimes forced into exile if they criticised the government however slightly, while dramatists were forbidden to mention any historical event that might, however indirectly, reflect adversely on the present régime. Many theatres were closed down. Others operated only under licence and were restricted to putting on a small repertory of officially sanctioned plays. One poet was consigned to detention in a mental asylum for writing: 'The great

Napoleon is a great chameleon', not because of its feebleness, but because of its sentiments! The same fate awaited any priest who spoke disparagingly of Napoleon from the pulpit. Artists, sculptors and architects got off more lightly – dictators always need the publicity offered by buildings, statues and pictures, the larger the better. Napoleon became a substantial spender on arches, pillars and monuments on the grand scale, but also, it is only fair to add, a judicious patron of the decorative arts in a style that still bears the name of 'Empire'. Fashionable artists such as David (see the illustration on page 142) and Ingres (see cover portrait) were employed by Napoleon as state propagandists, depicting him as a romantic hero-figure, or the embodiment of supreme imperial authority in classical guise, often complete with toga and laurel wreath. David as 'painter to the government' was given the oversight of all paintings done in France, with particular reference to the suitability of the subject matter.

iv) Education

Napoleon believed that there were two main functions to an education system. Firstly, it was to provide the state with a ready supply of civilian officials and administrators and loyal and disciplined army officers. He intended to recruit these from among the sons of the property-owning classes. Secondly, education had a clear role in binding the nation closer together – an aim that could only be fulfilled if the government took direct central control over the system.

Education for the common people was neglected by Napoleon, as it had been by the governments of the *ancien régime* and of the Revolution. All that was considered necessary for ordinary people was a simple 'moral education' and basic literacy and numeracy. This was provided in primary schools run by the Church, by the local community or by individuals. Napoleon often declared his belief in equal opportunities for all according to ability and irrespective of birth or wealth, what he called 'careers open to talents', but he generally failed to ensure that this was carried out in practice.

Secondary education was almost entirely restricted to the sons of *notables*. They were educated, often free of charge if their fathers were army officers, in the 45 highly selective, militarised *lycées* (elite schools) first introduced in 1802, and to a lesser extent to boys attending the rather less high-powered secondary schools established three years later. The system was highly centralised and government appointed teachers would all teach to a common syllabus from identical textbooks. So uniform was the system that Napoleon boasted that he knew exactly what every pupil in France was studying from the time of day. The *lycées* were one of Napoleon's permanent legacies.

Some areas of education were neglected. A similar provision was not made for the education of girls. Napoleon had a poor view of women, who 'should not be regarded as the equals of men; they are, in fact, mere machines to make children. I do not think we need bother about the education of girls ... Marriage is their destiny'. They did not, therefore, need to think and should not be taught to do so. Scientific study and research tended to decline after the *Polytechnique*, founded during the Revolution, was converted into a military academy in 1805.

In order to ensure that his wishes concerning education were complied with, Napoleon founded the Imperial University in 1808. This was not a university in the ordinary sense, but a kind of Ministry of Education developed from Napoleon's earlier 'Order of Teachers' and invested 'with sole responsibility for teaching and education throughout the Empire'. As Napoleon told the Council of State:

> Of all our institutions education is the most important. It is essential that the morals and the political ideas of the generation which is now growing up should no longer be dependent on the news of the day or the circumstances of the moment. We must secure unity; we must be able to cast a whole generation in the same mould. There will be no stability in the state until there is a body of teachers with fixed principles. Let us have a body of doctrine which does not vary and a body of teachers which does not die.

The University controlled the curricula and appointed all the teachers of the state secondary schools, which operated only by its permission and under its authority. Total obedience was demanded by the University from its member teachers, who had to take an oath of loyalty to their superiors, and were subject to many petty restrictions – a visit to Paris without special permission, for instance, would mean a spell in prison. Lessons were standardised, and what was taught was dictated in accordance with the needs and demands of the government.

There was no room for freedom of choice within the state system, nor for freedom of thought or expression by pupils or staff. For this reason many parents preferred to send their children, if they could, to the more expensive private Church schools especially when these became more easily available after the Concordat with the Pope in 1801.

v) Religion

As early as the summer of 1800 Napoleon was making proposals for some sort of accommodation with the Catholic Church in France, which had been in conflict with the state since 1790. Under the Directory, many parish churches had already been reopened and priests persuaded to officiate. It seems probable that matters had gone so far in the revival of Catholic public worship that no government could safely have ignored or opposed it, and that Napoleon' motives for seeking a *rapprochement* (restoration of friendly relations) with the Pope were those of expediency.

Napoleon had been born and brought up a Catholic but, as a good Jacobin, he had become if not exactly an atheist at least an agnostic. Although the Napoleonic legend was to have him die in the Catholic faith, he paid it no more than lip service during his adult life, and that only so that his coronation could follow the imperial tradition of Charlemagne (*c.* 742–814, King of the Franks and Holy Roman Emperor). However, he appreciated the power of religion to act as the 'social bond' cementing together a divided people, and the importance of its official re-establishment in bringing an end to the schism between clergy who had sworn allegiance to the Revolution and those who had not. Religious peace would help bring political and social peace to France. His opinion was that

> No society can exist without inequality of fortunes; and inequality of fortunes cannot exist without religion. When a man is dying of hunger beside another who is stuffing himself with food, he cannot accept this difference if there is not an authority who tells him, 'God wishes it so' ... It is religion alone that gives to the state a firm and durable support.

Catholicism had become identified with the royalist cause. It needed instead to be identified with the people as a whole. If it could then be reunited with the state, loyal in its support of the head of state and under his control, it would be a force for peace and stability in the country, and draw Catholics away from their Bourbon allegiance.

Having decided that 'the people need a religion', Napoleon set about 'rebuilding the altars', but with the proviso that 'this religion must be in the hands of the government'. Discussions with the papacy lasted many months and 21 different drafts were drawn up before the Concordat was finally signed on 15 July 1801. 'Nothing the *First Consul* had done was more controversial.'[7] The agreement confirmed that the separation of church and state, which had been one of the main policies of the revolution, was to end. On its side the Church recognised the Revolution and agreed that no attempt would be made to recover church lands. A state-controlled Church was established, and its clergy became paid civil servants, appointed by the government and bound to it by oath. While it was agreed that Catholic worship, 'the religion of the great majority of the citizens', should be 'freely exercised in France', it was also agreed that public worship should be 'in conformity with police regulations which the government shall deem necessary for public peace'. Napoleon also made it clear to all that there would be toleration for other faiths under the Concordat. He managed to achieve 'what no previous revolutionary regime had really wanted to bring about – the acceptance by the leadership of the Catholic Church of a government that was not led by a legitimate Bourbon prince'.[8]

The Concordat was published by Napoleon in April 1802 as part of a wide ranging ecclesiastical law on to which he tacked the so-called

'Organic Articles'. These were a series of articles limiting in every possible way Papal control over the French bishops, and increasing with equal thoroughness state control over the activities of the clergy as a whole. 'The Head of the Church', Napoleon announced, 'has in his wisdom and in the interests of the Church considered proposals dictated by the interests of the state ... What he has approved the government has listened to, and the legislature has made a law of the Republic'. He went on to exhort the clergy:

> See that this religion attaches you to the interests of the country. See that your teaching and your example shape young citizens in respect and affection for the authorities which have been created to protect and guide them. See that they learn from you that the God of Peace is also the God of war, and that He fights on the side of those who defend the independence and liberty of France.

In 1806 Napoleon went a step further. By standardising the numerous existing church catechisms (a series of questions and answers for teaching religious beliefs), he could turn a necessary ecclesiastical reform to political ends. The questions and answers of the new official catechism, as amended by Napoleon personally, were taught in all schools and carried a very clear message, one that was not at all agreeable to the Pope:

> Q. What are the duties of Christians towards princes who govern them? In particular what are our duties to Napoleon, our Emperor?
> A. Christians owe to the princes who govern them, and we, in particular owe to Napoleon I, our Emperor, our love and respect, obedience, loyalty and military service, and the taxes ordered for the defence of the Empire and his throne ...
> Q. Why are we bound in these duties to our Emperor?
> A. ... because God creates Empires and apportions them according to his will, and has set him up as our sovereign and made him the agent of his power, and his image on earth. So to honour and serve the Emperor is to honour and serve God himself ...

Napoleon also angered Pius VII by ordering, without reference to him, that the Church throughout the Empire should celebrate 16 August (the day after his own birthday) as St Napoléon's Day, unceremoniously removing from the calendar of saints the existing occupant of that date. The cult of the Emperor had reached its peak. Such blatant interference in church affairs for political and personal advantage made it obvious that Napoleon's religious activities were intended solely to produce loyal soldiers and civil servants. It was clear that the church was no longer the privileged First estate it had been under the *ancien régime* with its tax exemptions and vast landed estates. There appeared to be very little prospect that either would ever be restored.

3 The Hundred Days – a Change of Heart?

> **KEY ISSUE** In what ways did Napoleon signal his intention to change his approach to governing France during the Hundred Days' campaign?

When Napoleon returned to France in 1815 after his escape from exile in Elba (see page 130), he appeared to many to have changed his political beliefs. His new policies were a complete about turn – an unexpected shock to many old supporters, a pleasant surprise to most old enemies. Even before he reached Paris he had announced that he proposed to govern France constitutionally 'according to the interests and will of the nation'. Was he sincere in his proposals for a constitutional monarchy based on complete freedom of expression, a two-chamber parliament with an elected lower chamber and a hereditary peerage?

An astonished Benjamin Constant, his long-time liberal opponent who had warned Sieyès against Napoleon in 1799, was invited to draw up the *Acte Additionel* (or the *Benjamine* as the new constitution was nicknamed). After a long conversation in which Napoleon appears to have convinced Constant that he was sincere in wishing to 'give the people liberty' by introducing free elections, ministerial freedom of action, free discussion and a free press, the invitation was accepted. Constant justified his decision in a rather convoluted explanation that the Emperor was carrying out these 'democratic measures' while still 'in possession of the dictatorship, and at a time when, had the Emperor wished for despotism, he could have tried to retain it. It may be said', Constant continued, 'that such an attempt would not be in his interest – doubtless that is true; but is not that as much as to say that his interest accords with public liberty? and is not that a reason for confidence in his sincerity?'

There were other views. A staunch Bonapartist wrote:

> Whatever the personal prestige of the Emperor when defeated and dethroned, he was not the same man when he returned to power. He posed as a liberal, compulsorily, against his will, self-mutilated ... When even sincere Bonapartists cried 'We are your men, but on conditions: there must be no more despotism, but liberty, a constitution, guarantees' ... he was caught between two fires – that of his own nature and habits and that of the necessities of the situation – he was unmanned. He was no longer himself.

Fouché, the former Minister of Police, who had deserted Napoleon in 1814, was even more condemnatory:

> This man has been cured of nothing and returns as much a despot, as eager for conquests, in fact as mad as ever ... The whole of Europe will fall on him ...

The *Acte* was put to a plebiscite notable only for the massive abstention rate among the voters who had little enthusiasm for the 'new' Napoleon. Although he spoke publicly of the 1815 constitution as 'our rallying point, our pole star in hours of tempest', he seems privately to have regarded the *Acte* as simply a temporary concession to public opinion, a sop to the liberals without whose support he could not hope to rally the country to meet the coming Allied attack. Napoleon seems to have intended that the *Acte Additione* should be thought of not as a new constitution, but, as its name implied, an addition to the existing one. So he could, and did, claim that the proposed two-tier parliament of 1815 was not the result of a freestanding *Acte*, but the direct and logical development of the Napoleonic legislative bodies and the Senate. This in its turn enabled his supporters to claim that a liberal empire resulted naturally from an authoritarian state when the time was ripe. However, there seems little doubt that in reality Napoleon would, as he admitted later, have taken the opportunity of his first military victory to dismiss the parliament and return France to a dictatorship.

4 The Nature of the Napoleonic Régime

> **KEY ISSUE** What sort of régime did Napoleon establish in France?

What kind of régime was it that Napoleon had given France? While most historians would agree that Napoleon was a dictator, they might not go as far as Richard Cobb in describing the Empire as 'France's most appalling regime'.[9] It might be tempting to label Napoleon a military dictator, but is this accurate?

Napoleon had come to power by virtue of his reputation as a successful general and, at least until 1812, he retained the devotion of the ordinary soldier by virtue of his personal qualities of leadership, and his ability to win victories. From 1800 onwards there was what might be termed a certain 'militarisation' of society. With a general as head of state, and with universal conscription, it surprised no one that preference was shown to military personnel in awards of the Legion of Honour and of titles and estates, and that the *lycées* were organised along military lines. As the country was at war for most of Napoleon's time in power it was inevitable that the army should be very much in evidence, garrisoned in the towns or on the move along the roads – but at no time after the end of the *coup* was the army used by the government to interfere directly in politics, as had happened under the Directory. The role of the army at home was purely social. It took no part in implementing government policies and was not used by the authorities to control or intimidate the civilian population (apart from the suppression of unrest in the royalist west).

There was no large influx of military personnel into the administration either. Napoleon himself said to the Council of State in May 1802:

> I govern not as a general but because the nation believes that I have the qualities necessary to govern. If I did not have this opinion, the government would not survive. I knew full well what I was doing when as a general of the army, I accepted the position of member of he Institute ... We are thirty million men united by the Enlightenment, property-ownership and trade. Three or four hundred thousand soldiers are nothing compared with this great mass.

Felix Markham argues that describing Napoleon's regime as a military dictatorship is a distortion: 'It wouldn't have worked if it had been a military dictatorship. Napoleon's great strength in the Consulate was his ability to mobilize for his government all the men of talent. These included politicians and civil servants, many of whom were ex-revolutionaries or ex-*ancien régime* people. The fact that he was a soldier seems to be irrelevant: the whole point of the Consulate was that he proved himself a statesman as well as a soldier. So "military dictatorship" where the executive is run by generals and the army controls the state is rather a misnomer'.[10]

Nor was Napoleon's France a police state, governed by fear and repression although it is sometimes described as such. It is true that, apart from the Habsburg Empire, in no other state to date had the police played such a prominent part in society or had such all-embracing powers; but Napoleon's police bear little resemblance to the armed thugs of a modern police state. The general police might be sometimes arbitrary, sometimes brutal, but they did not, except on rare occasions, act outside the law. Only criminals needed to fear arrest. Much more dangerous, because more insidious, was the government control of private conduct and opinion through a network of informers of all kinds, some of them Fouché's, some Napoleon's. It was their presence that made life insecure for the many, and gave rise to the description of the régime as a police state.

Was Napoleon an 'Enlightened Despot'? Most historians would say no because, although he himself had been influenced in his youth by the Enlightenment, by its rationalism, its secularised society and its quasi-scientific principles, in later life he showed no sympathy for the political or moral ideas of the *philosophes* or *idéologues*. Many of them had supported the *coup d'état* of 1799, believing that Napoleon agreed with their liberal ideas on freedom and justice. They quickly discovered their error as they were manoeuvred out of political life, and one of the most intelligent and influential of them, Madame de Staël, was forced into exile.

Yet David Thompson suggests that his systematic reconstruction of the main legal, financial and administrative institutions of France 'gives Bonaparte a strong claim to be the last and greatest of the eighteenth-century benevolent despots.'[11] What grounds are there for this argument?

Many enlightened despots tended to concentrate on domestic reforms and peaceful policies rather than on foreign affairs and war, and in the early years of the Consulate, this was true of Napoleon. According to the *philosophes*, an enlightened despot should favour moderate government and should act rationally to reform the state. He should rule by good laws that would bring his people freedom and happiness. This could, however, only be done by the exercise of absolute power, because there was no other way of achieving practical results, but the ruler should have the welfare of his people always at heart.

It was during the period of comparative peace from 1800 to 1803 that Napoleon introduced many reforms and constitutional measures that once again made the French head of state an absolute ruler. Like many enlightened despots of the previous century he spoke publicly of the need for moderate government. He reorganised the country's finances, centralised the administration, curbed the power of the church (although he came to an understanding with the Pope in doing so), recodified the laws, reformed the judicial system and tinkered with education. Napoleon also built up the army – almost everywhere in the latter half of the eighteenth century the underlying motive of the enlightened ruler in embarking on his reforms was the establishment of his country as a military power. In 1803 war was resumed and was to occupy Napoleon to the exclusion of everything else for the remainder of his career; and enlightened despotism developed into dictatorship.

Some historians believe that from the first Napoleon had his sights set on dictatorship, perhaps even on the throne. Others would argue that this is doubtful, if only because he was an opportunist, not given to planning his actions any distance ahead but guided by changing circumstances.

In the first months after the *coup* the circumstances were not favourable to him. He knew that his hold on power was not strong. He was inexperienced in government. Napoleon, however, was very much a workaholic who put in long hours to understand how the wheels of government operated. He found it difficult to delegate decision-making to his ministers, preferring instead to keep as tight a control on policy-making as he could. He had to move with circumspection, not favouring one party against another, for he could easily be ousted in another *coup* if things went wrong. He had to win a convincing military victory quickly after Brumaire if he was to give stability to the new government and keep himself at the head of it. 'Conquest has made me what I am and conquest alone can maintain me'. The victory over the Austrians at Marengo in June 1800, and the peace treaties that followed, gave his personal prestige the boost it needed and made him and his government secure for the next 14 years.

References

1 Jean Tulard, *Napoleon: The Myth of the Savour* (Methuen, 1984) p. 81.
2 Albert Soboul, *The French Revolution 1787–1799: From the Storming of the Bastille to Napoleon* (Unwin, 1989) p. 547.
3 Martyn Lyons, *Napoleon Bonaparte and the Legacy of the French Revolution* (Macmillan, 1994) p. 73.
4 Vincent Cronin, *Napoleon* (Penguin, 1971) p. 253.
5 Richard Cobb, *The Police and the People: French Popular Protest 1789–1820* (Oxford, 1970) p. 115.
6 George Rudé, *Revolutionary Europe 1783–1815* (Fontana, 1981) p. 231.
7 William Doyle, *The Oxford History of the French Revolution* (OUP, 1989) p. 389.
8 Nigel Aston, *Religion and Revolution in France 1780–1804* (Macmillan, 2000) p. 333.
9 Richard Cobb, *The Police and the People*, p. 97.
10 Felix Markham, 'Napoleon and Europe', in *Nineteenth Century Europe* (Sussex Tapes, 1976) p. 35.
11 David Thomson, *Europe Since Napoleon* (Penguin, 1957) p. 57.

Summary Diagram
Napoleon and France: Politics and Power

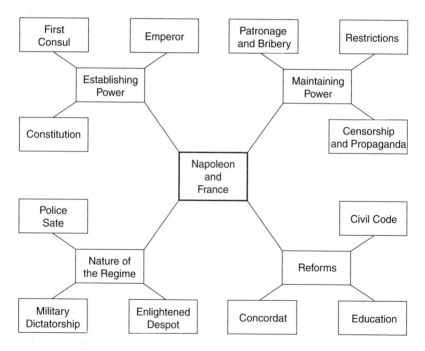

Working on Chapter 3

This is a long and detailed chapter that focuses on Napoleon's impact on the political, social and cultural life of France. Do not be daunted by it. If after your initial reading you find the content overwhelming revisit each individual section in turn and try to ensure that you grasp the main points. Use the sub-headings and numbered points to help you understand the most important aspects.

Answering structured and essay questions on Chapter 3

This chapter covers the whole span of Napoleon's rule over France, and as such the questions which are set will also span the whole period. Where there are two parts – **a** and **b**, it is possible that questions relating to **a** will require knowledge and understanding of specific measures, while those set in **b** will be much more open and will range across the period. The main issues are how did Napoleon establish power and how did he maintain his power once it was established. Another possible source of essay questions on this section could relate to the nature of the regime Napoleon created. The following are some examples that will require you to draw information from across the whole period.

The first part of a two-part structured question is designed to focus on some specific piece of information that you are required to explain before progressing on to the more analytical second part.

a) Explain the nature of two of Napoleon's domestic reforms. *(20 marks)*
b) 'Napoleon was only able to maintain power by means of repression.' How far do you agree with this statement? *(40 marks)*

For part **a**, you will need to provide a brief description of any two of Napoleon's domestic reforms, note who gained and who lost, how they were enforced and whether there was any opposition or support for them. In part **b** the answer will require you not only to consider carefully the validity of the view expressed in the statement but also to challenge it and present plausible alternatives. While a measure of repression was used, influential individuals were bound to the future of the regime by rewards and offices such as the Legion of Honour and the new imperial nobility.

Typical essay questions include the following:

1 'Napoleon's reforms were welcomed by all sections of French society.' Discuss.
2 'Napoleon's most significant domestic reform was the signing of the Concordat in 1801'. How valid is this interpretation of Napoleon's domestic policy?

3 How far did Napoleon's reforms during the Consulate bring benefits to all French people?

4 To what extent did Napoleon rule France with the consent of the people?

Remember to focus clearly on the question and to provide a measured and balanced response. You should avoid writing unnecessary narrative that does not relate directly to the question, and should direct your efforts to providing an analytical approach. A common theme with the first two questions is the provision of a bold/provocative statement which you are asked to consider. While there may be some element of support for each, there is also plenty to be critical about. Questions 3 and 4 suggest from the outset a more analytical and considered approach.

Source-based questions on Chapter 3

I Lucien Bonaparte and the Prefects

Read the extract on page 39, in which Lucien Bonaparate advises the prefects of their duties. Then answer the following questions:

a) What is meant by 'prefect' in the context of Napoleon's government? (*3 marks*)

b) Explain what Lucien considered to be the key elements of the role of the Prefects. (*7 marks*)

c) To what extent do you agree with the view that Napoleon's social and political reforms destroyed the ideals of Liberty and Equality promoted by the Revolution? (*15 marks*)

Napoleon and France: 'Son of the Revolution'?

KEY DATES

1789	14 July	Storming of the Bastille
	26 August	Declaration of the Rights of Man and Citizen
1792	10 August	Overthrow of the Monarchy
1793	6 April	Committee of Public Safety created
1794	27–28 July	*Coup* of Thermidor – Robespierre overthrown
1795	2 November	Directory established
1799	9–10 November	*Coup* of Brumaire
	December	Napoleon Appointed *First Consul*
1804	May	Napoleon proclaimed Emperor of the French
1806	21 November	Berlin Decree establishing the Continental System
1815	18 June	Battle of Waterloo
	17 October	Start of exile on St Helena in the south Atlantic
1821	5 May	Death of Napoleon, burial at St Helena

1 Napoleon and the Revolution

> **KEY ISSUE** What was Napoleon's view the French Revolution?

How can Napoleon's relationship to the Revolution be best described? Was he its heir, carrying on its policies and maintaining its ideals, or did he betray it and bring it to an end with a return to the policies of the *ancien régime*? Or was he, as he often declared, a bridge between the old and the new, combining the best of both worlds?

Napoleon's relationship with the Revolution was a changing one. It altered with the passage of time and according to circumstances. On a number of occasions in the early part of his career, he claimed to be a 'son of the Revolution', the staunch upholder of its principles and the inheritor of its teachings on liberty and equality. The proclamation of 15 December 1799, outlining the new Constitution, announced firmly that 'the Revolution has been stabilised on the principles which began it'. In 1800, with rather less revolutionary zeal and a more pragmatic approach, he told the Council of State:

> We have finished the romance of the Revolution. Now we must begin its history, looking only for what is real and possible in the application of its principles and not what is speculative and hypothetical. To pursue a different course today would be to philosophise, not govern.

After becoming Emperor he frequently promised that 'the French Revolution need fear nothing, since the throne of the Bourbons is occupied by a soldier', and at the end of 1812 he was still talking of his 'firm resolve to make the most of all that the Revolution had produced which was great and good'. However, his support for revolutions in general had waned:

> Since I have worn a crown I have shown clearly that I mean to close the doors against revolution. The sovereigns of Europe are indebted to me for stemming the revolutionary torrent which threatened their thrones.

He began to see himself as a personal peacemaker between revolutionaries and royalists: 'The greatest seigneurs [landowners] of the old régime now dine with former revolutionaries. My government has brought about this fusion'. In the same year, 1812, he addressed the Council of State on certain 'errors' made by the *idéologues* [thinkers] of the Revolution, 'to which every misfortune experienced by our beautiful France must be attributed'. He asked the Council:

> Who proclaimed the principle that rebellion was a duty? Who fawned on the people by proclaiming its sovereignty, which it was incapable of exercising? Who destroyed the awe and sanctity of the laws by making them depend, not on the sacred principles of justice, not on the natural order, not on civil law, but merely on the will of an assembly whose members were ignorant of civil, penal, administrative, political and military laws?
>
> He who has been called upon to regenerate a state must follow absolutely opposite principles.

In exile at St Helena, however, he sought in his *Mémoriale* to justify his actions and policies and to almost reinvent himself as the great defender of the Revolution and guardian of its achievements, the 'prince of liberal opinions':

Let me charge you to respect liberty; and above all equality. With regard to liberty, it might be possible to restrain it in a case of extremity ... but heaven forbid that we should ever infringe upon equality! It is the passion of the age; and I wish to continue to be the man of the age!

The great battle of the century had been won and the Revolution accomplished; now all that remained was to reconcile it with all that it had not destroyed. That task belonged to me. I became the arch of the alliance between the old and the new, the natural mediator between the old and the new orders. I maintained the principles and possessed the confidence of the one; I had identified myself with the other. I belonged to them both ... I closed the gulf of anarchy and cleared away the chaos. I purified the Revolution, dignified nations and established kings. I excited every kind of emulation, rewarded every kind of merit, and extended the limits of glory.

Napoleon had been an army officer, aged 20, when the Revolution began in 1789. He was immediately caught up in the excitement and became an ardent patriot, although his enthusiasm was temporarily dampened in August 1792 after witnessing the storming of the Tuileries, and the massacre that followed (his life-long fear of crowds is generally thought to date from this time). Much later he expressed the view that a revolution however justified 'is one of the greatest evils by which mankind can be visited' because of the violence and suffering it brings in its train, but he was able to console himself by reaffirming his belief that 'The Emperor [by his policies] has healed the wounds which the Revolution inflicted'.

The importance of the property-owning classes, both established landowners and those who had benefited from the purchase of *biens nationaux* (church land) during the Revolution, was clear to Napoleon. Property figures prominently among the revolutionary principles on which the Constitution of 1799 was alleged to be founded. These were listed not, as in 1789, as liberty, equality, fraternity, but as representative government, the sacred rights of property, equality and liberty. It is worth nothing that the 1799 Constitution avoids any explicit reference to the *Rights of Man and of the Citizen* (1789) and that fraternity has disappeared from it altogether, while equality and liberty (in that order) are preceded by property. Napoleon asserted over and over again that the preservation of liberty and equality were at all times his chief concern, but his actions too often belied his words for his excuses about extreme pressure of circumstances did not carry much weight with his critics. He insisted that he maintained the principles and preserved the positive gains of the Revolution; but how far did his domestic policies actually accord with his declared Revolutionary ideals? Did some of his reforms – restoring the position of the Catholic Church, reviving the aristocracy – in fact suggest a flavour of the *ancien régime*?

2 Revolutionary Ideals in Practice?

> **KEY ISSUE** Did Napoleon preserve or destroy the revolution?

Napoleon may have put 'representative government' as the first revolutionary principle of his 1799 Constitution, but he was at pains to ensure by means of his new 'electoral' systems that it would not be effectively implemented, nor would executive power be divided.

a) Government and Administration

There is evidence to suggest that in some ways Brumaire did not mark a clean break, as was once thought, between the Directory and the Consulate. Research has been undertaken into the composition of the legislative bodies, the central bureaucracy and the provincial administration of the Consulate. This indicates a continuity of personnel from pre-Brumairean days. Of the first 300 members of the Legislature, for instance, 240 had been members of the Directory councils, as had been 69 of the 100 first members of the Tribunate. Most of the first holders of senior administrative posts had been in office at the time of the *coup*. They were just taken over by the new régime, and this link with the past helped to stabilise Napoleon's government in its early days. In provincial administration, 76 of the first prefects appointed had been members of various Revolutionary assemblies. Most of them were in their mid-forties, many with considerable experience as ministers or high-ranking executives during the previous decade.

The Council of State chosen, appointed and presided over by Napoleon, had at the end of 1799 a membership of 29, all of whom were men of high ability and half of whom were well experienced in government service under the Directory. The Council, which was a consultative not an executive body, was used by Napoleon, especially during the Consulate, to bypass the Legislature by issuing Orders in Council. The various ministers were subordinated to it, and therefore to Napoleon himself, and their activities were co-ordinated through the Secretariat (later the Ministry) of State, an institution itself taken over from the Directory. There were continuities of staff and organisational similarities from the Directory and the *ancien régime* to be found in Napoleon's government structure.

The key features of the new political structure were:

- A Council of state chosen by the *First Consul* – this was similar to the old Royal Council by which the kings of France had governed.
- Government-appointed officials (prefects, sub-prefects and mayors) replaced the devolved, locally elected but inefficient system of local government favoured by the Directory.

- Napoleon retained the *départements* of the Revolution, but reintroduced the 40,000 pre-1789 communes as his basic territorial and 'electoral' unit.
- The prefect's role was an important one, the link between the people and the ruler. It is often likened to that of the *intendant* (local royal official of the *ancien régime*) whose powers had been limited by the authority of the *parlements* and Provincial Estates. No such curbs existed for the prefect.
- The provincial judicature became similarly centralised when appointed judges replaced the elected ones of the Revolution and new Courts of Appeal were established.
- Direct tax collection was also reorganised centrally and local tax-collectors appointed for the purpose.

Once the Consulate was made hereditary it became to all intents and purposes a monarchy. Napoleon, despite his revolutionary past, openly admired certain aspects of the Bourbon régime and described 'the old administration ... [as] the most perfect that ever existed'. He saw the Revolution as entirely compatible with monarchy and believed that if Louis XVI had been more adaptable he could have remained king. As it was, his death left the way open for Napoleon to 'pick a crown out of the gutter' and establish the 'fourth dynasty of France'. In 1804 Napoleon became 'by the grace of God and the Constitution, Emperor of the French' – he seems to have decided against adopting the title 'King of France' in deference to revolutionary sensibilities, and to avoid a direct comparison with the monarchical past. In any case his ambitions had outgrown the idea of a mere kingdom; he already saw himself at the head of a 'universal empire'.

This might all seem a far cry from the doctrines of 1789, but it is possible to argue otherwise. By retaining the words *'République Francaise'* on official documents until 1804 and on the reverse of his coins until 1809, Napoleon was demonstrating to the people that his government, both Consulate and Empire, was a continuation of the Revolution. On the other hand, when, after his consecration by the Pope, Napoleon took the crown from the altar, raised it above the congregation and placed it on his own head, he was showing that sovereignty no longer belonged to the people as in republican days but had been transferred absolutely to him and his heirs for ever. It is possible that the coronation ceremony was the result of family pressure on Napoleon to found a hereditary dynasty, with all the advantages this would bring to his brothers and sisters in the way of titles and lands. Less convincingly it could be seen as a conciliatory gesture to royalists and a means of encouraging their acceptance of the new emperor in place of the old king; or, rather more probably, as a bid for equality and respectability among the crowned heads of Europe. The presence of the Pope at Notre Dame certainly gave Napoleon a prestige he could not otherwise have acquired, while making it plain to the rest of the world that the Church had given its blessing to an Empire sprung from a Revolution it had previously denounced. Indeed, on the eve of the Austrian marriage in 1810 (which itself was seen by many Frenchmen as a betrayal of the Revolution) Napoleon, entertaining what he called a 'garden of kings', presented himself to them as a fellow monarch welcoming his royal neighbours.

The lack of any popular representation in either of his régimes would not have worried Napoleon, for his view of sovereignty of the people had become far removed from that of Rousseau's *Social Contract*, a classic statement on the principles of republican government that had much influenced Napoleon's political ideas as a young man. By 1804 Napoleon considered that sovereignty of the people in no way implied the right of the people to a say in government, but simply gave them the right to have a ruler who governed them as the majority of them wished to be governed – and that he had fulfilled his obligations by giving them the strong, autocratic government he believed most of them wanted or needed. In a way, the Napoleonic Empire was like an absolute monarchy but under another name. In the decree of 1808, which established the imperial nobility, Napoleon referred to the people not as citizens, but as his subjects. 'Sovereignty, after its selective association with "the nation" or "the people" at different times during the Revolution, had once again become identified in a person'.[1]

b) Equality?

The abolition by the Revolution of feudal and other dues and services was confirmed by Napoleon, and equality before the law was more or less preserved in his Civil Code. The rights to the ownership of property in general, and to the continued enjoyment of *biens nationaux* acquired during the Revolution in particular, were also safeguarded. In the eyes of many contemporaries, the award of honours, and of titles, marked a clear break by Napoleon with the Revolution (see page 35). The creation of an elite was considered prejudicial to the idea of equality. Napoleon tried to justify his actions by pointing out that the titles carried no legal privileges or tax immunity, and that by establishing a nobility based on service to the state, not on birth, he had destroyed the old aristocracy. Yet this argument was somewhat undermined by the fact that the newly ennobled could buy an entail (property) and make their titles hereditary. In answer to criticisms of the Legion of Honour he spoke, equally unconvincingly, of it as a 'unique decoration', and of 'the universality of its application as the symbol of equality', and explained how 'I instituted the new nobility ... to satisfy the people, as the greatest part of those I ennobled sprang from them – every private soldier had a right to expect he could earn the title of duke'.

Is the old textbook cliché correct in claiming that Napoleon reconciled the aristocracy of the *ancien régime* with the bourgeoisie of the Revolution to form a new governing élite, which even men of humble origins could also aspire to join – the so-called 'politics of amalgamation'? Napoleon established the imperial nobility in 1808. By 1814 more than 3200 imperial titles had been created (the majority between 1808 and 1811). A total of 20% of the Napoleonic aristocracy were ordinary people ennobled for military service, 22% came from the old nobility, but the overwhelming majority – 58% – came from the ranks of the bourgeoisie.[2] Studies of the composition of lists of members of the Tribunate and Legislature have given rather similar results and seem to bear out the textbook statements. However, historians working on the membership of the *arondissement* and departmental electoral colleges have painted a different picture, with a far smaller percentage of old nobility and a much higher proportion of businessmen among the members. Research on the lists of notables (the wealthy) drawn up by the prefects in each department has found that in this setting there were comparatively few men of humble origin. The majority were members of the bourgeoisie, and the remainder former nobles – few of whom actually accepted office under Napoleon. Despite all the research, the precise composition of Napoleon's governing élite is still uncertain, but what is clear is that the bourgeoisie were the dominant element. Jean Tulard considered that the formation of a new imperial nobility in 1808 was a decisive turning point, which marked the beginning of the end of the Napoleonic Empire since it represented a violation of the egalitarian principles of the Revolution.[3]

One of Napoleon's favourite remarks was that he followed faithfully the Revolutionary ideal that talent and courage should be rewarded without distinction of birth, 'provided they have the knowledge, the ability and the qualities'. This was a considerable exaggeration. As the new nobility could buy hereditary rights, so could money buy privilege and position. Without money, or at least influence and the right connections, there was little chance of much advancement in any sphere. The opportunities for improving their social and economic status seem to have been extremely limited for agricultural workers. A few managed to acquire a small plot of land, although seldom enough to support a family, especially as the land that became available after 1800 was usually of very poor quality. It was apparently a good deal easier for artisans to move into the urban lower middle class and set up a small business, although they were unlikely to be able to develop it very far because the business world was largely in the hands of only a few, well-established families, many of whom had risen to prominence through the world of banking.

In the professions, too, the way to the top was barred. There were large numbers of poorly paid posts in the bureaucracy. Without good educational qualifications, however, there was no hope of promotion and to get such qualifications was not easy for those of humble origin. Sons of officers could be educated free in the *lycées*, but others had to pay. Church-run private schools were expensive, primary schools were almost non-existent and the people as a whole were illiterate. There were clearly strict educational limits to the 'career open to talents'. Clerks in the bureaucracy did not become heads of department, nor heads of department become ministers. Even in cases where the young man of good family had completed a course in the *lycée* he might find that this was not enough. The Audit Office, established in 1803 as a training ground for young recruits aspiring to the highest government posts, required candidates for appointment to it to have an income of 6000 francs a year. As one candidate for a job complained, this 'officially removed from the rank of auditor all less well-off young men, however well educated, however gifted, hardworking and well bred they may be'. Too often in practice it was promotion by seniority not merit and, given Napoleon's preference for obedient servants rather than independent thinkers, the best did not always reach the top.

In the army promotion for a conscripted peasant was difficult, and the chances of reaching any rank higher than that of lieutenant extremely remote. The exceptions, men like Ney and Murat who rose to be marshals, can be counted on the fingers of one hand. A fair number of Napoleon's generals were from military families and of noble origin, but most came from the bourgeoisie. Despite the saying attributed to Napoleon that every soldier carried a field-marshal's baton in his knapsack, no private soldier ever found one there.

Even in the matter of conscription there was inequality of opportunity to avoid it. The proportion of young men liable for call up varied from region to region, an arrangement that was clearly unfair. The reasons for the variations were usually political or military – the Vendée, for instance, with its strongly royalist tradition was favourably treated in the hope of mollifying its inhabitants, while frontier departments in the east and open to foreign attack were up to five times more heavily assessed. In addition, under a law passed in 1800, a rich man could avoid conscription by paying a substitute to serve in his place, and between five and 10% of those conscripted did so. As time went by and losses in battle rose, so too did the price of substitutes. By 1811 even the poorest peasant needed a substantial inducement to join the army, and the price reached a figure of about nine times the annual income of an unskilled labourer.

Taxation was another area of inequality. The Directory had revived the pre-revolutionary practice of levying indirect taxes, but it was the Empire that expanded them to provide the major part of the revenue needed to pay for the war. On the grounds of good financial practice, the burden of taxation was increasingly shifted from direct to indirect taxation – that is from the well-to-do property-owners to the consumers, the majority of whom were poor. Taxes on land rose only slowly, while the yield of indirect taxes increased by 50% in the decade to 1814. In 1802 taxes on tobacco, playing cards, alcohol and some other goods were regrouped into the unpopular *droits réunis*. In 1806 a tax on salt, unpleasantly reminiscent of the *gabelle* of the *ancien régime*, was introduced, and four years later the old state monopoly on tobacco was re-established.

c) Liberty?

During the Hundred Days Napoleon, in the course of a long conversation with Benjamin Constant, defended his past illiberal actions on the grounds of political necessity. 'I am not an enemy of liberty', he said, '[but] I set it aside when it obstructed my way'. And set it aside he did, restricting liberty of action and freedom of expression, moulding thought and belief, and imposing absolute political authority. His law codes, particularly the Criminal and Penal Codes, were much closer to the practices of the *ancien régime* than to those of the Revolution. The use of censorship and propaganda, the practice of indoctrination in the *lycées* and via the Imperial Catechism, the activities of the spy network and of the police, all played a part in the establishment and maintenance of the Napoleonic state – at the expense of liberty.

In 1814 when Napoleon was facing the Allied invasion of France – the first time foreign troops had been on French soil since 1793 – his advisers begged him to call on the memories of those Revolutionary days and rally the people to the country's defence. 'How can I', said Napoleon, 'when I myself have destroyed the Revolution?'

d) Evaluation

Napoleon's own preference was always for authoritarian rule – 'I do not believe that the French love liberty and equality', he told the Council of State in 1802. 'Ten years of revolution has not changed them'. As Consul Napoleon 'mingled the qualities of republican hero and bourgeois king with those despotic and uncontrollable traits which his personality already possessed'.[4] He himself had little time for representative bodies, but he seems to have felt a sense of guilt about his failure to govern with the aid of a parliament of the kind that he admired in England. Successive Revolutionary governments had made all posts open to direct election. Popular participation, though, had been disappointing, with voting levels low, and there was little public protest when Napoleon abolished elections for all administrative and judicial posts. Officials of all kinds (even JPs from 1806) were subsequently appointed instead, most of them chosen by Napoleon himself from names on the electoral college lists. Napoleon's France was an autocracy operated through a centralised and efficient bureaucracy.

Napoleon's domestic policy in many areas was not only a move away from the ideals of the Revolution and a reversion to at least some of the practices of the *ancien régime*, it was also a foretaste of the dictatorships of the twentieth century. Napoleonic France may not have been a military dictatorship directly under the control of the army but it was certainly a militaristic state, geared to war and conquest, and the army had considerable prestige and influence. To Napoleon *la gloire* was as important as it had been to Louis XIV a century earlier and territorial expansion as important as it was to be to Hitler a century later. For all three rulers the achievement of these ambitions was dependent upon their absolute authority at home. Napoleon expressed this openly when he spoke of his desire for 'the empire of the world' and how, in order to ensure it, 'unlimited power was necessary to me'.

'Napoleon: reformer, revolutionary or reactionary?' is an old question to which there is no clear answer. The centralisation of government, for instance, can be seen either as a reform of the loose control exercised by the Directory, or as the first steps to absolutism and a return to pre-Revolutionary days, while the Civil Code can be judged either a completion of the unifying work begun during the Revolution or a reactionary set of Articles restoring the paternal authority of Roman Law. Perhaps it is more realistic to say that Napoleon, as an opportunist, assumed a variety of guises – reformer, revolutionary or reactionary as best suited him at the time. Not surprisingly, therefore, several of his institutions represent a pragmatic compromise between the Revolution and the *ancien régime* – the Concordat, for example, officially abandoned the Revolutionary anti-clerical line, while at the same time obtaining official Papal recognition that the sale of church lands was irrevocable. The conclusion of Richard Cobb and Colin Jones is:

> Although Napoleon consolidated many of the Revolution's achievements, including administrative and legal changes, economic reforms and the abolition of feudalism, much of what was most distinctive and significant about those years perished at his hands. The Rights of Man were turned on their head as discipline, hierarchy and authoritarianism replaced the revolutionary device of liberty, equality and fraternity. Under his rule France passed into the hands of an autocrat with far more absolute power than Louis XVI had ever enjoyed.[5]

3 Napoleon's Impact on France

KEY ISSUES How much did France change in the years from 1799 to 1815 under Napoleon's rule? What impact did he have on the country, and how long did it last?

It was at one time generally accepted that remarkable and far-reaching changes were made in France by Napoleon. At present there is less certainty regarding this. There is consensus that continuity with the Revolution and/or with the *ancien régime* was much greater than previously believed, that France changed less in the Napoleonic period than during the shorter Revolutionary one, and that comparatively little of Napoleon's work outlived his régime. What is the evidence?

Of course there *were* changes – political, constitutional, legal and religious – under Napoleon, which affected, by his direct intent, the way individuals thought and the way they lived; and there were other of his activities, his obsession with war for instance, which affected society more indirectly. The impact of some changes outlasted the Napoleonic era, while others did not.

Napoleon's governmental and administrative reforms replaced the popular sovereignty of the Revolution (loosely controlled, devolved government based on a system of elections) with a centralised autocratic rule not unlike that of the *ancien régime*, especially after the establishment of the Empire in 1804. His legal and judicial reforms were based on the authoritarianism of Roman law, while his suppression of freedom of expression and his extension of police powers smacked more of the Bourbon monarchy than of the Revolution. In present-day terminology, Napoleon's human rights record was not good. Behaviour was regimented and beliefs were moulded through education, propaganda and censorship. Opposition was vigorously rooted out. Life was geared to the service of the state and its ruler in a way never previously seen in France, even in the time of Louis XIV. It would be easy, though, to exaggerate the repressive nature of Napoleon's rule and to forget that (even allowing for the fact that it would have been almost impossible in practice for him to have put them into reverse) he *did* maintain the great gains of the Revolution. He confirmed in the Constitution and the Civil Code, the end of feudalism in France and the equality of Frenchmen before the law, and in the Concordat the irrevocability of the sale of the *biens nationaux*. What were the more general effects of Napoleon on France?

a) Social impact

Our knowledge of social conditions, especially among the poor, in Napoleonic France is patchy and inconclusive. Comparatively little research has been done on the less wealthy elements of society in either town or country.

From those local studies that have been carried out it seems that agricultural wages rose only slowly in the years 1800–15 and hardly kept pace with prices and rents. The latter rose sharply due to the increased demand for land. The reasons for this increased demand are uncertain. It may have been a consequence of the increase in population. Where land *did* become available for purchase, only holdings of poor quality and under five hectares in area were within the peasants' financial grasp. All the better land was bought up by members of the bourgeoisie; but, having acquired it, they did little with it, regarding its possession simply as a status symbol and a sound investment. There was no agricultural revolution at this time and farming continued in the old unimproved subsistence tradition. This may have been partly because, until 1811, the harvests were particularly good. Food was therefore plentiful and cheap and the people were reasonably content. It was not until the bad harvest of 1811, followed by the extra conscription burdens of 1812–14, that Napoleon was faced with any serious social unrest.

Despite the good harvests and the end of feudalism, there seems to have been at least as much rural poverty in the later years of the Empire as there had been before 1789; but the situation was patchy, and in some regions, particularly the cereal-growing areas of the north, contemporaries reported an overall improvement in peasant dress, housing and diet.

Napoleon was politically so committed to the beneficiaries of the Revolution, such as the bourgeoisie who had bought land, that his social policies were of the most conservative kind in relation to the rural and urban poor. He liked to speak of how the French people loved him as the 'People's King' or as the peasants' friend, but it is difficult to see why either he or they should have believed it. He did nothing for the mass of the people except take their sons for the army and tax them for its support. The continual levying of young men and the markedly more efficient arrangements for the collection of taxes directly affected the peasants much more than any other class of society. Yet they were the ones who cheered his return from Elba in 1815. He ascribed their support to the rapport that he said had always existed between him and his peasants. It seems more likely that their continued support was based on the fear that feudalism would return along with the Bourbons. After 1815 the mythical figure of the 'Emperor of the common man' was created by the Napoleonic propaganda machine as a reaction to Bourbon favouritism towards the aristocracy.

So few statistics are available about the urban working class that it is unclear whether there was a shortage of labour in the towns caused by the war, or whether, on the contrary, there as an excess of labour brought about by an influx of peasants from the countryside and of deserters from the army. Either way, conditions for workers were bad, particularly after the ban on workers' coalitions (early trade unions) was reaffirmed in 1803 and, although there is little information on exactly how much the *livret* (see glossary) was used, it must always have threatened a worker's right to seek new employment. Napoleon seems to have regarded the urban workers with the gravest suspicion, believing them to be troublemakers who needed firm handling and close police supervision.

Even the more prosperous elements of society are not well understood. Although a good deal of research has been done, most of it has been concerned with investigations into the composition of the Napoleonic élite based on lists prepared by prefects and others, most of which provide no more than name, wealth and occupation and tell us nothing about the people, their families and how they lived.

What effect did Napoleon's long wars have on the population of France? The slow growth rate of the French population, in comparison with that of other western European countries during the nineteenth century, used to be attributed to the heavy loss of life among young men drafted into his army. Recent demographic research suggests, however, that this explanation is inadequate because the fall in the birth-rate had begun even before the Revolution.

For reasons not entirely understood, young people began to marry earlier from the late 1780s onwards, but at the same time to have smaller families. The earlier marriage can be explained after 1792 by the young men's anxiety to avoid conscription, but the fall by some 20% in the birth rate in the last quarter of the eighteenth century is more difficult to understand. It is suggested that after 1789, with the reduction of traditional moral pressures from the church and society, birth control came to be widely practised, and that the series of economic catastrophes during the 1790s together with the Revolutionary laws on property inheritance (*partage*) may also have helped to keep families small.

Did Napoleon's wars have an effect on population growth? The answer would appear to be, yes, but to a much lesser extent than was at one time believed. Of the 2 million men who found themselves in the army between 1800 and 1814 the number killed (dying of wounds, disease, hunger or cold, or who simply went missing believed killed) has been estimated at 916,000. This figure is usually quoted as representing about 7% of the total population of France; but that is misleading because the losses were not spread evenly across the population. They fell heavily on the young men of marriageable age – a devastating 38% of men born in the years 1790–5 were killed, the majority of them between 1812 and 1814. To the extent that this must have left many young women without husbands, and have reduced further the already declining birth rate, Napoleon's wars must accept some responsibility for the slow growth of the population in nineteenth-century France.

b) Economic impact

Opinions differ over whether or not the French economy expanded or stood still under Napoleon. There are also rival views over whether or not France benefited or suffered under the Continental Blockade (see page 112).

i) Industry

In 1785 the economic development of Britain and France was comparable. But in the next 15 years, while Britain was forging ahead in industrial development, the upheavals of the Revolution held France back. While Cobban's view that under Napoleon the only 'trade which flourished was smuggling', might on reflection appear rather harsh, the message from the industrial sector during the Empire was mixed.[6] Some sectors of the French economy were probably on the edge of an industrial revolution by 1800. In the cotton industry the number of cotton-spinning firms in Paris doubled between 1803 and 1806, tripled between 1806 and 1808 and nearly doubled again to 57 between 1808 and 1811.[7] In 1807 there were over 12,000 workers employed in the industry in Paris. French imports of raw cotton more than doubled between 1803 and 1807, and a shortage of supplies from French colonies was made up until 1811 by overland shipments from the Levant (the eastern Mediterranean) that entered France through Strasbourg.

This dramatic growth was due to mechanisation of spinning by the introduction of imitation British 'mule-jennies' (mechanised spinning machines) and by the protectionist effect of the Continental Blockade on home production that removed the competition from British cotton cloth. But, despite its expansion, cotton did not become a factory-based industry – it remained a cottage one. Even in the largest spinning firm, 90% of its 8000 employees were scattered round Paris as home outworkers, and the same was true on the weaving side of the industry. There was no similar advance in any of the other textile industries. Linen and hemp manufacturers found themselves facing declining demand and the silk and woollen industries suffered also from the fashionable preference for cotton dress materials during the Empire.

Other industries, too, developed only slowly in the Napoleonic period. The chemical industry did make some progress, developing artificial dyes and new bleaching materials for the cotton spinners and weavers, and experimenting with the production of artificial soda for the soap manufacturers of Marseilles. The iron industry benefited from the demand for armaments needed for Napoleon's wars, but failed to modernise itself, preferring the old method of smelting the ore with charcoal rather than coal.

Across industry as a whole there is little evidence that in the early 1800s France was on the verge of an industrial revolution of the kind experienced in Britain. While Napoleon is said to have been keenly interested in French industry and to have provided manufacturers with substantial subsidies, it does not appear to have been one of his priorities. Georges Lefebvre said that as a soldier Napoleon's preference was for 'an agricultural and peasant society; the idea of a society dominated by a capitalist economy was unsympathetic, if not even alien, to him.'[8]

The economy of the countryside was equally stagnant. Despite official encouragement, land clearing and drainage made little headway. Yields did not increase and labour methods remained primitive. Landowners did not reinvest their rents in the land and no new techniques were developed. Any agricultural expansion that took place was simply an extension of the cultivated area. The only other development of any significance was a government programme for the growing of sugar-beet and chicory to fill gaps left by the colonially produced sugar and coffee no longer available under the rigours of the Continental Blockade. To sum up: 'The years from 1800 to 1815 were thus characterized by the juxtaposition of a rural economy of ancient type hardly yet modified, a seaport economy stifled after a century of expansion, and an industrial economy whose leading sectors could not yet activate the general forces of production, and which presents the image of a brilliant, but localized success'.[9]

ii) The Continental System and Blockade 1806–13

The Continental Blockade was a two-pronged enterprise, a combined 'war-machine' and a 'market-design', intended to double as an economic weapon against Britain and as a commercial shield for France.

In November 1806 Napoleon announced by the Berlin Decrees that the British Isles was officially in a state of blockade by land and sea and forbade any communication with them by France or any of her satellites. This was in response to a British naval blockade of the French coast, which had begun a few months earlier in May 1806. Early in 1807 the British extended their blockade. Neutral ships were required to call at British ports for inspection, to pay duties and to obtain licences, before trading with French controlled ports. At the end of 1807 Napoleon countered with the Milan Decrees. These extended the embargo on British goods to all neutral ships that complied with the new British demands.

The Blockade was an ambitious plan to conquer Britain by economic means. British exports and re-exports were to be prevented from leaving the country and the unsold goods would then build up to such an extent that British trade would be brought to a standstill and her economy disrupted. If, at the same time *imports* into Britain were allowed, or even encouraged – on condition of cash payment in gold – this would help to drain away her bullion reserves and weaken her economy further. She would become unable to fulfil her main role in the Coalition against France – that of providing the ready money needed to maintain and equip the allied armies – and might well decide to settle for a separate peace before her position as a trading nation had been totally undermined.

The Blockade as a 'market-design' was intended to protect French home industries from British competition and to provide them with new European markets in the satellite and annexed states. In return these states would provide goods needed by France for home consumption or manufacture and re-export to the rest of the Empire. In this way Napoleon's European territories would form a self-sufficient commercial and trading enterprise, independent of foreign goods.

How well did these arrangements work for Napoleon? From the start the operation of the 'war-machine' suffered from the lack of French sea power. The situation worsened after most of the navy was destroyed at Trafalgar in 1805, and with an ineffective navy and an incompetent and corrupt customs service, smuggling became widespread. In 1809, in an attempt to regularise the situation, increase customs revenues and get rid of a surplus of wine and grain stocks, Napoleon took drastic action against smugglers. He seized and destroyed contraband goods, and instituted a system of licences enabling French subjects to trade with the enemy. These new measures, by reducing opportunities for illicit trading with the continent, had a serious effect on the British economy. By 1811 Britain, in difficulties from the failed harvest of 1810 and the need to pay in gold for shipments of grain exported under licence from France, and with her own overseas trade lower than at any time since 1802, faced a potentially disastrous crisis in her balance of payments. The Blockade had been more successful as an economic weapon against Britain than is usually accepted. Without the catastrophe of the French invasion of Russia (itself a byproduct of the Blockade), Britain's prospects would have been bleak; but by 1813 Napoleon, desperately in need of money to finance a new campaign, was issuing so many licences that the Blockade was no longer of any significance as an economic weapon of war.

What were the effects of the Blockade on France? British historians have tended to concentrate on the maritime aspects, and this has led to a rather unbalanced view of what is a much more complex situation. French historians have looked more at the general economic effects and it now seems that the effect of the Blockade on France was a mixed one.

There is no doubt that the ports of the Atlantic and Channel coasts did suffer quite severely from the loss of sea-borne trade, and from the British navy's counter-blockading activities. Shipbuilding and its associated maritime trades, such as rope-making and sail-making, declined and so too did inland industries that depended on overseas markets. The old established linen industries of the north and west of France, for instance, already in decline and technologically backward, were badly affected by the loss of exports. With the decline in opportunities for overseas trade and the consequent loss of profits, many of the older industries suffered from lack of capital. This underfunding was made more acute when many investors moved their money out of commercial enterprises into what now seemed to be the better security of land ownership. In consequence, several of the old merchant families and banking houses collapsed due to a general lack of business confidence.

All was not doom and gloom, however, for in some areas, well away from the Coasts, French subjects positively benefited for a time from the protection to home industries that the Blockade offered, and by the opportunity it provided to export goods across the Alps and the Rhine to outlying parts of the Empire. There the inhabitants, unable to buy legitimately elsewhere, had no choice but to pay the high prices demanded by French producers. As the British navy increasingly barred the sea-lanes to French goods, trade routes moved overland, away from the coast. Paris became an important trading centre for luxuries, and items of fashion, as did Lyons for silk goods. Strasbourg and other eastern frontier cities prospered as entrepôts (ports where merchandise could be temporarily stored) as the Rhine traffic and the trade it provided in both legitimate and contraband goods more than doubled in the years 1806–10.

Attempting to enforce the Blockade throughout Europe pushed the country into disastrous new conflicts, notably in Spain and Russia, leaving France weakened militarily, economically and politically and Napoleon's fortunes in decline. This partly led to the bourgeoisie's withdrawal of support for Napoleon. In 1810 the French economy was facing a severe crisis. Among the contributory factors to this were the cost of Napoleon's wars, which had become more expensive and less profitable, over-speculation in goods smuggled through the blockade, a public panic to unload old, soon-to-be worthless coins and the hoarding of new-minted francs. To compound the crisis, several banking houses outside France in which Parisian bankers had invested heavily collapsed. Many small firms had borrowed large sums from the banks to survive, as the costs of raw materials rose. When their loans were called in they could not repay their debts and widespread bankruptcies followed. Unemployment rose steeply throughout France.

The 1811 harvest was very poor and resulted in a sharp rise in food prices, over 50% in most areas. To try to help the situation the government introduced controls on grain and on the sale of bread. Millions of bowls of free vegetable soup and bread substitutes were distributed in an attempt to tackle the crisis, but not until the harvest of 1812 did the situation begin to improve for the majority of people.

Most of the bourgeoisie ignored the original causes of the economic crisis as well as the effect of natural disasters in prolonging it – apart from the bad harvest, there had been a cyclone that devastated the silk-producing areas. Instead they put all blame and responsibility for the depression of 1810–11 directly on the workings of the Continental Blockade, and therefore on Napoleon who had introduced it. They had begun by approving his protectionist policy as being to their advantage, but when it no longer proved profitable to them, they abandoned him. He had lost his chief supporters. Even when he more or less abandoned the Blockade by extending special export licences, they did not return to his side, but remained markedly indifferent to his subsequent fate and to that of his régime in 1814.

c) Cultural impact

Culturally Napoleon's legacy to France is not inspiring. Even allowing for the stifling effect of his policies of propaganda and indoctrination, he was not much concerned with the arts, literature, sculpture, painting or drama, except in so far as they glorified himself. 'Napoleon's censorship hurt both the periodical and book trade more than any regime before it.'[10] He closed down most of the theatres in Paris but, rather strangely, took the company of the *Théâtre Francaise* with him to Moscow in 1812. Paris itself changed little under Napoleon. Apart from the addition of a number of triumphal monuments in classical style – the Arc de Triomphe itself, and the column in the Place Vendôme that bears a statue of Napoleon in a toga, for instance – it remained in appearance the city of Louis XVI.

The style of the years 1800–15, never called 'Napoleonic' but always 'Empire' (perhaps to emphasise the importance of official art), is seen at its most distinctive in the context of interior decoration where it directly reflects Napoleon's own interests. Its inspiration was from the classical world of Greece and Rome (shades of Alexander and Caesar) or from Egypt, where Napoleon in 1798–9 had uncharacteristically concerned himself as much with deciphering the country's ancient heritage as with the process of conquering it. Inlaid furniture, decorated with mythological figures of all kinds and military emblems, was very much the rage, as were the new, tall looking-glasses seen everywhere. Antiquity, with a touch of the east, dominated not only furnishings but the Empire style of dress favoured by everyone in society except Napoleon. Without regard to fashion he continued to wear, except on state occasions, a battered hat, a long grey overcoat and the green jacket of the Imperial Guard.

d) Impact on the frontiers of France

By the time of Brumaire 'old' France had grown considerably in the ten years since 1789 and with each successive year Napoleon pushed the sphere of French influence further beyond the 'natural frontiers' of the Alps, Pyrenees and Rhine, annexing some states, and turning others into French satellites until in 1811 the Empire reached its greatest extent (see the map on page 119).

Was this expansion in the interests of France or not? The Revolutionary governments had fought since 1792 for foreign recognition of France's 'natural frontiers', which would provide clearly defined and easily defensible borders. Until Napoleon's first Italian campaign, the Republic had not envisaged permanent involvement beyond them.

One of the main aims of eighteenth-century diplomacy had been to maintain the balance of power, allowing no one country to dominate all others. Conquests had been returned or divided up between interested parties at the end of a war in order to keep a balance among the major powers. By retaining control over his Italian conquests in 1797 at the peace of Campo Formio instead of arranging an exchange of territory, Napoleon set a pattern of expansion for the future, by which, as far as he was concerned, a French conquest remained a conquest. In addition, many Churches and Treasuries in the conquered territories were stripped of works of art and bullion that were shipped back to France. 'In 1796 Bonaparte remitted [sent] something like 45 millions [in bullion] to Paris.'[11] He never willingly parted with any conquered territory – there could be no negotiated peace settlement to restore a pre-war balance of power. That was never his understanding of the purpose of war. As a result, he committed France to further wars in defence of each new conquered territory, in the course of which more lands would be conquered. This remained the pattern while Napoleon continued winning. After the defeats of 1812–13 the structure started to unravel.

Continuous war necessarily imposed a strain on French resources, both as regards men and materials. In the days of the Consulate and the early Empire the burdens of conscription and taxation, though heavy, were not excessive. Only about half the men conscripted were actually enrolled in the army – the remainder were exempted because they were married, were only sons, were physically unfit or for other reasons. The shortfall was made up with auxiliary troops supplied by the satellite countries. In the same way the level of taxation could be kept down, for much of the cost of the war was met by tribute payments from the same source. After 1812 and the disastrous invasion of Russia the situation changed. With the loss of the Empire the whole burden of raising and maintaining army after army fell on France. Taxation rose sharply – by between 50 and 100% – at a time when many incomes had fallen as a result of the 1810–11 depression. Conscription of yet another army at the end of 1813 to replace that lost at the battle of Leipzig ran into such difficulties that married men were no longer allowed to claim exemption. Some young men even practiced self-mutilation to avoid military service.

Could the Empire be said to have been of any practical benefit to France itself? It is difficult to find much economic benefit, apart from the acquisition of the Rhineland. This area, where there was comparatively rapid industrial development, soon became the most economically advanced part of France, and its loss in 1815 was a serious blow. For a while from 1806 the protectionist policies of the Continental Blockade brought some commercial advantages to France, but it did not last and any other profit from the annexed and satellite states was swallowed up, and more, by the cost of continued war. Napoleon had envisaged a self-sufficient Empire, providing for France as well as itself. Events proved him to have been over-optimistic. The prestige of having the largest European Empire since that of Rome was no compensation to most French subjects for the problems of maintaining it. The glory was bought at too high a price.

Napoleonic France came to an end in 1815. The first Treaty of Paris (1814) pushed the frontiers of France back to those of 1792, the second Treaty of Paris pushed them back to 1790. There was nothing left of the imperial possessions. Even the 'natural frontiers' were lost. In territorial terms no trace of the Empire survived.

4 Napoleon's Legacy: What Survived After 1815?

> **KEY ISSUE** Did any of Napoleon's policies and achievements survive his defeat in 1815?

Some of Napoleon's innovations disappeared because they were inappropriate to the succeeding régime – Louis XVIII, given a free hand, would also probably have preferred to rule as an absolute monarch, but pressure from the allies forced him to give France a limited constitution. Napoleon's centralised and autocratic government structure therefore disappeared, along with the imperial title, in favour of a (nominally) representative government. However, other institutions remained, including much of his bureaucratic organisation, which had increased rapidly in size by 1815. The Ministry of the Interior, for instance, which enjoyed very wide-ranging powers, over-seeing provincial administration, trade, arts and crafts, prisons, public works, education, science, welfare and a host of other topics, had proliferated into a number of departments and bureaux with an ever increasing staff to match. Other civil ministries, a dozen or more of them, had expanded equally rapidly to meet the needs of a government perpetually at war, doubling their staff to a total of around 4000 by the late Empire. On the basis of this well-organised civil service, headed by specially selected and trained auditors, Napoleon could be described as 'the originator of modern centralised bureaucracy in France'.

Members of the imperial nobility kept their titles at the Restoration, the Legion of Honour continued to be awarded, Frenchmen remained equal before the law, and the land settlement was left untouched. The legal codes and much of their judicial organisation remained in being. Today, judges are still appointed for life and the *Code Napoléon* is still the foundation of modern French law, although it was recodified in 1958. The provincial administrative system of prefects, sub-prefects and mayors is still the basis of local government. Most of Napoleon's financial reforms survived, including the Bank of France. So too did the *lycées*, in a demilitarised form; and the Baccalaureate examination introduced in 1809 is still sat by French children at the end of their school life. Although the University itself expired with the Empire, its purpose of supervising and standardising education throughout the country lives on, as does its structure of advanced academies, seen in the modern centralisation of French higher education. In religious life, the Concordat, minus the Imperial Catechism, remained the basis of relations between the French government and the Roman Catholic Church until 1904 when it came to an end with an agreement that totally separated Church and State. In the same year government financial support for Protestant ministers was finally abandoned, as was the government oversight of Jewish synagogues. One or two other innovations, smaller and less important, also survived from the Napoleonic régime. These included the local workers' arbitration board (*conseil de prud'hommes*) that played a significant part in industrial relations.

Essentially Napoleon's legacy to France was a civil one. From more than a decade of war he left his country no permanent reminder – except a few triumphal arches, civic names and the Legion of Honour. Whether the overall effect of Napoleon's rule on France was for good or ill is debatable – the strong government, the good order, the glory and prestige that he gave the country must be balanced against the restriction of freedom, and the cost of war, in terms of human suffering and economic hardship, that his régime imposed on the French people. Any judgement on this topic must, of course, reflect the values of the individual making it.

References

1 Geoffrey Ellis, (Longman, 1997) p. 53.
2 Martin Lyons, *Napoleon Bonaparte and the Legacy of the French Revolution* (Macmillan, 1994) p. 171.
3 Jean Tulard, *Napoleon: The Myth of the Saviour* (Methuen, 1985) p. 253.
4 François Furet, *The French Revolution 1770–1814* (Blackwell, 1988) p. 219.
5 Richard Cobb and Colin Jones (eds), *The French Revolution: Voices from a Momentous Epoch 1789–1795* (Simon & Schuster, 1988) p. 242.
6 Alfred Cobban, *The Social Interpretation of the French Revolution* (Cambridge, 1964) p. 74.
7 D.M.G. Sutherland, *France 1789–1815: Revolution and Counterrevolution* (Fontana, 1985) p. 382.
8 George Lefebvre, *Annals Historiques de la Révolution française*, No. 119 (1950) p. 276.
9 Louis Bergeron, *France Under Napoleon* (Princeton, 1981) p. 159.
10 Emmet Kennedy, *A Cultural History of the French Revolution* (Yale, 1989) p. 23.
11 William Doyle, *The Oxford History of the French Revolution* (Oxford, 1989) p. 358.

Summary Diagram
Napoleon and France: 'Son of the Revolution'?

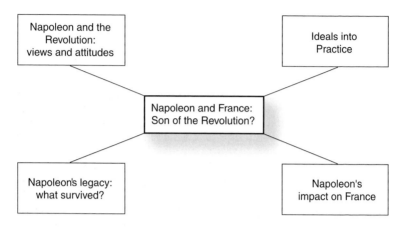

Napoleon and France:
Son of the Revolution?

Working on Chapter 4

This long chapter in essence considers a central issue relating to Napoleon and France, namely to what extent can he be considered a 'son of the Revolution'? Did he, in fact, preserve any of the gains of the Revolution? Any analysis will need to balance Napoleon's own interpretation of his policies and achievements against the views of historians. His own views contain not only an element of self-justification but also more than a hint of propaganda. Discovering the truth is not an easy task but it is one which you will need to attempt. To support your understanding you may well find it useful to construct a two-column grid. In one column try to identify aspects of the revolution that Napoleon preserved, while in the other note those that he abandoned and/or destroyed.

Answering structured and essay questions on Chapter 4

Questions on this topic will tend to focus mainly on the central issue of whether Napoleon preserved or destroyed the gains of the Revolution. Following your reading of this chapter, you should now be familiar with the main areas of policy under consideration, and you will be aware that there is no simple or clear answer to this question. It is possible to make convincing arguments for either interpretation. The reality, you will probably decide, lies somewhere between the two extremes and is a combination of both.

Study the following structured question:

a) Choose any two of Napoleon's domestic reforms and outline briefly what they did. *(10 marks)*
b) Who benefited and who lost as a consequence of the two reforms you have identified in a)? *(15 marks)*
c) To what extent is it accurate to say that Napoleon was a son of the Revolution? *(25 marks)*

Parts **a** and **b** will require you to focus on two reforms, for example the Concordat or the political changes. In **a** you will only be required to deploy factual information relating to each measure – what they did or how they operated. For part **b** you will need to provide an evaluation relating to who gained and who lost as a consequence of each reform. Ensure that you address each reform in a balanced and fair way and that you answer the question in an analytical manner. You will need to spend at least half of the allotted time on part **c**. The contents you will be expected to draw upon will range across the period from 1789 to 1815. In order to consider the validity or otherwise of this view, you will need to consider Napoleon's remarkable progress during the revolution before the *coup* of Brumaire before evaluating his policies as *First Consul* and later Emperor.

Consider also the following essay questions:

1 Do you agree that Napoleon's domestic policy succeeded because it was largely a return to the ideals of the *ancien regime*?
2 How far did Napoleon's reorganisation of France fulfill, and how far distort, the aims of the Revolution?
3 'Nothing more than a dictatorship.' How far do you agree with this assessment of Napoleon's rule of France?
4 'Napoleon secured and retained power in France through the use of force'. Discuss.
5 'I am the French Revolution and I must defend it.' How valid is Napoleon's view of his role during the period 1799–1815?

These questions all relate to Napoleon's domestic policy but do not focus on any single specific measure. When you revise Napoleon's domestic policy ensure that you cover all the key aspects – political, social, economic, cultural and religious. You may not need to deploy all these aspect in every question. A good introduction that relates clearly to the question is recommended; depending on the nature of the question you may then want to produce an argument in support of the question, then a counter argument before providing a balanced conclusion that summarises your views regarding the question.

Source-based questions on Chapter 4

1 Critical Historical Voices

Read the extract from Richard Cobb and Colin Jones on page 62 and then answer the questions that follow:

a) What is meant by 'economic reforms' in the context of Napoleon's government of France? (*5 marks*)

b) Explain why 'The Rights of Man were turned on their head'. (*10 marks*)

c) 'Napoleon's social and political reforms destroyed the Revolution's ideals of Liberty and equality.' Explain why you agree or disagree with this view. (*25 marks*)

2 Napoleon on St Helena

Read the extract on page 55 that Napoleon dictated while in exile on St Helena, and answer the questions which follow:

a) Explain the meaning of the phrase 'I became the arch of the alliance between the old and the new' (line 7). (*5 marks*)

b) What do you think Napoleon meant when he says that: 'The great battle of the century had been won and the Revolution accomplished'? (*10 marks*)

c) In the source, what does Napoleon suggest has been his great achievement? (*15 marks*)

d) To what extent can Napoleon's interpretation of his achievement be considered to be fair and accurate? Explain your answer. (*25 marks*)

5 Napoleon and Europe: Conquest

POINTS TO CONSIDER

For many, the most memorable of Napoleon's achievements are his military conquests, which laid the basis of his empire in Europe. This chapter will deal with two main areas: firstly the campaigns Napoleon fought in Italy and Egypt as a soldier of the Directory, and then those he oversaw during the Consulate and early Empire. A string of stunning victories laid the basis of one of the largest European Empires of modern times. Another area for you to consider is how Napoleon was able to achieve his remarkable successes. In order to evaluate this you will need to note carefully the various factors that contributed to the victories – among them, qualities of leadership, the development of new tactics and strategies, and advances in weaponry and training. During your first reading of the chapter, familiarise yourself with the main campaigns and, in general terms, with how they were won.

KEY DATES

1796	23 February	Napoleon given command of the Army of Italy
1797	October	Peace of Campo Formio
1798	19 May	Napoleon embarks on Egyptian expedition
	1 August	French fleet destroyed by Nelson at Aboukir Bay
1799	22 August	Napoleon leaves Egypt, abandoning his army
1800	June	Battle of Marengo
1801	9 February	Peace of Lunville with Austria
1802	25 March	Peace of Amiens with Britain
1803	May	War resumes with Britain
1805	20 October	Austrian army defeated at Ulm
	21 October	French fleet defeated at Trafalgar by Nelson
	2 December	Austrian and Russian forces defeated at Austerlitz
	26 December	Peace of Pressberg with Austria
1806	15 September	Prussia joins Britain and Russia against Napoleon
	14 October	Prussian armies destroyed at Jena
1807	June	Russia defeated at battle of Friedland
	7–9 July	Treaty of Tilsit between France, Prussia and Russia

1 The Early Campaigns – Italy and Egypt 1796–9

> **KEY ISSUE** How successful were Napoleon's early campaigns?

It was the Italian campaigns of 1796–7, with a dozen victories in less than a year, that made Napoleon's name as a general. They not only set the seal on his military reputation, but provided the starting point for the legend. As a result, much of what has been written about the campaigns, by Napoleon and others, is a fanciful embellishment of the facts. The oft-repeated account of how a young, insignificant general who was very much a political appointee dramatically won over to his side the sceptical veteran officers of the Army of Italy is a considerable exaggeration. Napoleon was already well known to the officers concerned, and they, far from deriding him, seem to have welcomed him on his arrival as the man most likely to lead them to victory. There is no official record of the rousing piece of oratory that he is alleged to have delivered as his first speech to the army, and that appears in the St Helena account. Instead of the colourful promises of 'rich provinces and great cities which will be in your power' together with 'honour and glory when I lead you into the most fertile plains in the world', there was in reality only a rather staid and mundane order of the day. The army itself is commonly described as dispirited and demoralised, so making Napoleon's achievement in bringing it speedily up to scratch appear all the greater. In fact, although the army had not had much success since 1792 and was badly clothed and fed (mainly because of corrupt administration), it consisted of experienced and hardened campaigners, mostly volunteers or regulars, and its discipline and morale were generally good. All it needed was inspiring leadership, and this Napoleon provided.

Within a month of his arrival in Italy he had conquered and occupied Piedmont, and at the beginning of May 1796 was crossing the River Po in pursuit of the Austrian army into Lombardy. He seems to have regarded the subsequent battle of Lodi and the entry into Milan as a psychological turning point in his career. Following these victories, which gave him a degree of confidence, Napoleon believed that he could 'perform great things, which hitherto had been only a fantastic dream'. Italy lay wide open to the plundering French soldiers as they marched south defeating four separate Austrian armies as they went. In February 1797, with the capture of Mantua, the French conquest of northern Italy was complete.

Napoleon next moved against Austria itself and a month later was only just over 60 miles from Vienna where, with his army exhausted and dangerously far from base, he offered the Austrians preliminary peace terms. While these terms were awaiting ratification, Napoleon completed his triumphant Italian campaign by occupying the

Republic of Genoa (which adopted a French-style constitution and became the Ligurian Republic), by overrunning part of the Republic of Venice and by concluding on his own initiative an agreement with the Pope. He then installed himself and his wife Josephine in near-royal splendour in a castle near Milan.

The Treaty of Campo Formio (October 1797), negotiated by Napoleon, consolidated French gains into the newly formed Cisalpine Republic (Modena, Ferrara, Reggio, Bolgna and the Romagna, with the addition of Lombardy and the former Venetian possessions of the Ionian islands and part of Dalmatia). One of Napoleon's central aims in his negotiations with the Austrians was to establish French control of the Mediterranean.[1] Part of this strategy was the acquisition of the Ionian Islands as trading bases. The new vassal state was given a system of government based on the French constitution of 1795 and its executive and legislative bodies were nominated by Napoleon himself. 'Only he can make peace, and he can do it on any terms he wants' was the comment of one Austrian envoy in Paris. It seemed a brilliant peace from the point of view of French national prestige and was received as such in Paris where Napoleon was given a hero's welcome.

The need to keep this ambitious and potentially dangerous young man and his unemployed troops busy, and out of politics, was clearly a factor in the Directory agreeing to send him with the Army of the Orient to invade Egypt. Napoleon for his part hoped to attack British commerce and trade in the east. Despite the early loss of his fleet, destroyed by Nelson in Aboukir Bay in July 1798, which cut the 'Army of the Orient' off from France, Napoleon again distinguished himself in the field at the battle of the Pyramids. Egypt was quickly occupied but an advance into Syria was ultimately less successful. Napoleon, over-confident after capturing Jaffa, blundered badly at the siege of Acre. After losing half his men, he gave up the attempt to capture the fortress and returned to Egypt. There he received news that sent him hurrying back to France in August 1799. (The army, so embarrassingly abandoned, managed somehow to survive without him until its final defeat in 1801 by a British expeditionary force.)

i) Assessment

The campaigns in Italy and to a lesser extent in Egypt were a foretaste of what was to come. Militarily, they showed Napoleon at his best, and are a model for later *blitzkrieg* (war of rapid movement) strategies that he used so successfully until 1808 to defeat his enemies' old-fashioned and disunited armies. They are illuminating in other ways too, for they show that many of the personality traits that came to be associated with Napoleon were already well established – among them, great personal ambition, supreme self-confidence, determination and ruthlessness, as well as undisputed powers of leadership. He frequently exceeded his orders, particularly when negotiating peace

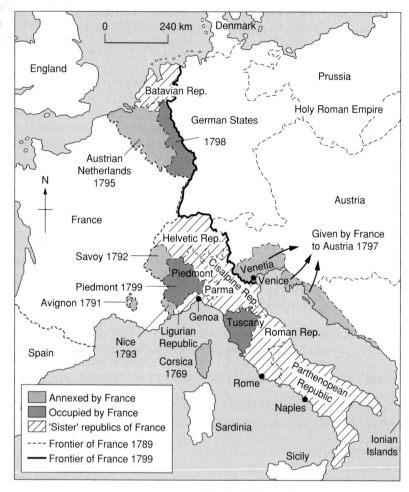

France and Italy 1799

terms with defeated enemies, and could be guilty of unnecessary cruelty, as can be seen by his order of the cold-blooded murder of 3000 prisoners after the fall of Jaffa.

The 150 scholars and scientific experts who accompanied him to Egypt did excellent work, but his motives for taking them are not entirely clear. He may have been genuinely interested, especially as he had just been made a member of the *Institut de France*, and it is true that Egyptian influence was later to feature in the Empire style of furniture and interior decoration, but his propaganda at the time suggests, rather, that he was thinking of himself as a modern day Alexander or Julius Caesar, combining military success with learning in the course of founding a new empire.

2 Wars of the Consulate and Early Empire 1800–7

> **KEY ISSUES** What was the extent of Napoleon's military victories during the period 1800–7? What were the consequences of these victories for France?

The need for an early victory and a quick peace after the *coup d'état* of November 1799 in order to strengthen his own position as *First Consul* led Napoleon back to Italy. There in June 1800, after a march across the Alps, he inflicted a decisive defeat on the Austrians at Marengo. A further French victory at Hohenlinden in Bavaria six months later brought about the peace of Lunéville. It recognised French possession of Belgium (the Austrian Netherlands) as well as the left bank of the Rhine and the gains in Italy. Austria lost control of all northern Italy, except Venetia, and her influence in Germany was reduced. With the collapse of the Second Coalition Britain agreed to the Peace of Amiens (March 1802), by which France withdrew from the Papal States and Naples, and Britain returned most of her conquests including Egypt, which was restored to the Ottoman Empire.

The peace settlement proved to be unstable, a mere truce in a war that had already been going on for almost a decade. After a period of increasingly acrimonious relations between France and Britain over breaches of the spirit if not the letter of the peace treaty on both sides, war broke out again in May 1803. Mastery on land lay with France, dominance at sea with Britain. Neither in itself was sufficient for victory. Napoleon tried to remedy this at the end of 1803 by the assembly of a fleet and a vast army at Boulogne. There for the next two years both remained poised for an invasion of England. The invasion plans came to nothing, mainly because Napoleon would not admit that his knowledge of naval matters was rudimentary. He had no understanding of the sea or its ways, nor of the importance of wind and weather in the deployment of sailing ships. By insisting, for instance, against all advice, that the fleet put to sea for a review on a day when a storm was brewing, he caused great disorder and damage among the ships. His whole plan for the invasion was unsound, depending not only on suitable weather conditions, but also on the unlikely event of effecting at the same time a French command of the sea for long enough to transport the army across the Channel. The idea had to be abandoned in October 1805 when Nelson's victory at Trafalgar destroyed the combined Franco-Spanish fleet, needed to lure the British ships away from the Channel, before it could reach the scene of operations. Even before this French disaster, Napoleon had gathered up his Army of England and marched south to the Danube to confront Austria, which had declared war on France during the summer.

The campaigns of 1805–7 that followed Napoleon's departure from Boulogne showed him at his military best, winning a series of crushing victories against the armies of Austria, Prussia and Russia. The latest incompetent Austrian general was outmanoeuvred and forced to surrender at Ulm in October 1805. The defeat of an Austro-Russian army at Austerlitz in December caused Russia to retreat rapidly out of Napoleon's reach and Austria to agree to the treaty of Pressburg, which recognised French supremacy in northern Italy and the loss of Austrian authority in Germany. Complicated negotiations between Napoleon and Prussia, involving Prussia's acquisition of Hanover in return for adherence to Napoleon's Continental Blockade, led to a breakdown of relations and then to war between the two countries. In a remarkable one-week campaign Napoleon destroyed Prussia at the twin battles of Jena-Auerstädt (October 1806). In February 1807 Napoleon marched through Poland to attack Russia, his remaining continental enemy, winning a technical victory over the Russians in the bitter battle of Eylau. A major defeat at Friedland in June convinced the Russians of the need to make peace. This was done in July 1807 at Tilsit in a personal

'The plumb-pudding in danger' by James Gilray, published 26 February 1805. Britain and France divide up the world.

meeting between Napoleon and Tsar Alexander I. This took place initially on a raft in the middle of the River Niemen, which marked the Russian frontier.

i) Assessment

In two years (1805–7) and a series of short campaigns, Napoleon had in turn defeated three of his four opponents. In November 1806 he established the Continental Blockade to deal with the remaining one, Britain, who had taken no active part in the war, restricting herself to supplying her allies with subsidies. His achievements were truly astounding. These were:

- French domination in Germany by defeating Austria and abolishing the Holy Roman Empire.
- Confederation of the Rhine created as a French satellite state.
- Prussian power destroyed and Prussian Poland converted into the Grand Duchy of Warsaw.
- Prussia's lands in the west created into the new satellite kingdom of Westphalia.
- Napoleon crowned himself King of Italy, and added Parma and Tuscany to the existing French possessions of Piedmont and Lombardy, and made Naples into a French satellite.
- Russia was forced to conclude peace in 1807, and Tsar Alexander compelled to make a formal alliance with France.

By the end of the year Napoleon controlled directly or indirectly the greater part of Europe. The 'Grand Empire' had come into being.

3 | Military and Strategic Developments

> **KEY ISSUES** What military and strategic developments was
> Napoleon responsible for? How did these contribute to his
> victories between 1800 and 1807? What other factors contributed
> to Napoleon's military success?

a) Napoleon's Qualities of Leadership

One of Napoleon's great strengths as leader was the devotion of his men. His soldiers adored him. Why was this?

Napoleon possessed enormous self-belief. In 1804 he wrote: 'I am destined to change the face of the world; at least, I believe so. Perhaps some ideas of fatalism are mingled with this thought, but I do not reject them; I even believe in them, and this confidence gives me the means of success.' According to François Furet, Napoleon's 'most important secret was his genius for action and tireless energy, which he threw into dominating the world.'[2] Despite his generally unprepossessing appearance, when he wished to charm he could quickly win over anyone he met, however initially hostile they might be. His contemporaries had no doubt about the charismatic quality of his leadership. His great adversary Wellington said of him that the moral effect of his presence in the field was worth an additional force of 40,000 men to the French army. This he ascribed partly to Napoleon's dual position as both head of state and commander-in-chief that gave him unparalleled control over events, but also to his great personal popularity with the army. *The Times*, in its obituary notice of July 1821, remarked that 'He had the art, in an eminent degree, of inciting the emulation and gaining the affections of his troops'.

By the use of theatrical and emotional language in his Bulletins and Orders of the Day Napoleon formed a special bond between himself and the army. He played on the ideas of military glory, of patriotism and of comradeship, while giving at the same time the impression that he had a deep paternal concern for his men. To this they responded with real devotion. 'The Emperor', he wrote for example in a Bulletin in 1805, 'is among you. He sets the example; he is on horseback day and night; he is amongst his troops, wherever his presence is necessary'. Later in the same campaign he set out to rally the men by allying himself with them: 'Whatever the obstacles we meet we shall overcome them, and we shall not rest until we have planted our banners on the territory of the enemy'. The same campaign finally over, there was a judicious use of praise and promises. 'Soldiers! I am very pleased with you. Today at Austerlitz you have proved that you have the courage which I knew you had ... I shall lead you back to France and there I shall do all I can to take care of your interests.' Sometimes he played on their greed with promises of material reward in the form of loot. As he said, 'The most important quality in a general is to know the character of his soldiers and to gain their confidence. The military are a Freemasonry, and I am their Grand Master'.

So great was Napoleon's charisma, even in the dark days of 1812, that a sergeant in the Imperial Guard, describing the chaos, suffering and heartbreak of the retreat from Moscow by the tattered, frost-bitten remnants of the *Grande Armée*, could afterwards write of himself and those with him:

> They walked – on frozen feet, leaning on sticks – silently, without complaining, men of all the nations making up our army, covered with cloaks and coats all torn and burnt, wrapped in bits of cloth, in sheepskins, in anything to keep out the cold, holding themselves as ready as they could for any possible struggle with the enemy ... The Emperor in our midst – on foot, his baton in his hand ... he so great, who had made us all so proud of him, inspired us by his glance in this hour of misfortune with confidence and courage, and would find resource to save us yet. There he was – always the great genius; however miserable we might be, with him we were always sure of victory in the end.

Great as his powers of leadership were, they alone could not have won his battles. There are other factors to be considered.

b) The Changing Nature of War

The majority of eighteenth-century wars were fought with more or less evenly matched, mainly mercenary armies, very similar to each other in training, equipment, composition and strength. Each was quite small, containing sometimes as few as 30,000 men, and the wars were normally undertaken with limited objectives such as the acquisition of a small province, more often than not to be eventually returned after use as a bargaining counter in maintaining the balance of power in the game of international diplomacy.

The great military theorist of the early nineteenth century, the Prussian von Clausewitz, had fought in the Revolutionary and Napoleonic wars. In his classic book *On War* published in 1832 he put forward his view that 1793 marked a turning point in the organisation of armies and in the conduct of war. He considered that both were changed forever by the creation in that year of the French 'nation in arms' (the *levée en masse*) that transformed limited war into total war:

> Perfected by Napoleon, military power based on the strength of the whole nation marched over Europe, smashing everything in pieces so surely and certainly, that where it only encountered the old-fashioned armies, the result was not doubtful for a moment. [3]

The cry of *la patrie en danger* ('the nation in danger') had led in 1792 to the formation of a French national army consisting initially of 'patriotic volunteers'. Universal conscription had long been advocated by such different men as Guibert (the influential and aristocratic pre-Revolutionary military reformer) and Rousseau (the equally influential eighteenth-century philosopher). Both thought it the best way to raise a citizen army that would have wide support, and in 1793 conscription was actually introduced. A year later there were a million men under arms. (France had the advantage of having at that time the largest population in Europe, about 28 million, from which to draw recruits.) Although in practice the large majority of conscripts were from poor peasant families, in theory at least universal conscription brought together men from all classes of society in defence of *la patrie*. [4]

Eighteenth-century generals tried to avoid battle, if at all possible, concentrating instead on sieges, or on manoeuvring in order to evade the enemy or to gain a tactical advantage – what Clausewitz called 'diplomacy intensified, a somewhat more vigorous way of negotiating'. Violence was controlled by calm calculation of the risks involved and careful observance of the conventions of war. The *élan* (enthusiasm and passionate commitment) of the Revolutionary armies was something alien to established military practice. The men fighting in the new

French armies were not there as mercenaries, not as men impressed against their will, but as citizens honourably defending *their* Revolution against its threatened destruction by outside forces. Instead of avoiding battle they actively sought it. Often ill-disciplined and ill-equipped, they relied on shock tactics and the momentum of the bayonet charge to bring them success, especially in their early encounters.

The year 1793 was a watershed in other ways than the introduction of conscription – it marked the first *amalgame*, the merging of remnants of the old army with the new. The introduction of veteran soldiers into the new army did much to bring order into its early chaotic organisation without destroying its verve, and formed it into a fighting force that Napoleon used as the basis of his *Grande Armée*. Napoleon therefore inherited significant developments that had been introduced by the Republic, and which he subsequently built upon.

c) The Development of the Grande Armée

In the four years of comparative peace between 1801 and 1805 Napoleon organised the French armies according to a pattern which was to be adopted by all European forces for the next century and a half, 'one which made possible almost unlimited decentralization under a single command'.[5] His new arrangements were based on the ideas of Guibert, whose thinking was probably the single most important influence on Napoleon's military development. The whole army was divided into corps of about 25,000–30,000 men each composed of two or three divisions, infantry and cavalry; some of the cavalry were kept separate, as were the reserve artillery and several élite groups, the most important of which was the Imperial Guard. The entire army was under the direct and sole control of Napoleon himself, as the commanding general.

The organisational aim was to allow unity of command – Napoleon's – while providing flexibility in action. Each corps was given a particular role on a campaign march, but this role could if necessary be quickly changed; regiments could be transferred from one corps to another if required, and infantry or cavalry detachments could be sent out as skirmishers or moved round as protective screens to shield the movements of the rest of the troops, and leave the enemy confused and uncertain as to what was happening. In battle as well as on the march, flexibility was the key. Once the engagement was joined, the idea was to manoeuvre in the way that would best lure the enemy into taking up an unfavourable position, and then tempt him into committing his whole force, including his reserve, into an all-out attack. Napoleon would at this point order his own reserves to launch a surprise enveloping attack on the enemy's rear and/or flank. In the decisive French charges and relentless pursuit that followed, heavy casualties would be inflicted on the fleeing enemy. These casualties sometimes, as at Marengo, Ulm, Austerlitz and Jena, numbered three times as many as those suffered by the French. This strategy was not new. It had been proposed many years earlier by Guibert, but this does not belittle the brilliance of Napoleon's early victories. To win them he took what had been only a military theory and successfully put it into practice. As Napoleon himself said, 'everything is in the execution'.

d) The Development of Winning Tactics

For some time before the Revolution, military strategists had argued about the best way to deploy the principal part of the army, the infantry, on the march and in battle. Should they be in line or column? The column, a long file of soldiers moving slowly along a single road, was the traditional marching formation, but was extremely vulnerable to enemy attack and almost powerless to take offensive action in an emergency. The line abreast was the equally traditional battle formation, three more or less stationary ranks of musketeers firing continuously to order. Well trained, disciplined troops could be very effective in this formation against infantry or cavalry, but were always vulnerable to concentrated artillery fire.

In 1791 a compromise was reached between the 'column or line' schools of thought, and embodied in a new drill manual. This allowed the commander to choose whatever combination of line and column seemed best to him at the time, in what came to be called 'mixed order'. It was a development of this 'mixed order' that Napoleon most frequently employed in battle – the infantry in a concentrated but mobile formation made up of both line and column, moving around the battlefield as required, firing at will, and following up, in Revolutionary tradition, with a massed bayonet charge when needed, and supported by the cavalry.

On the march Napoleon dispersed his forces into self-contained groups advancing simultaneously at a distance of perhaps as much as a mile from each other along several roads, in effect forming a series of columns in line abreast. This allowed for mutual support and reinforcement in case of attack and at the same time simplified the requisitioning of supplies from the countryside through which the army was passing. Following Guibert's precepts once again, Napoleon ensured that the army should travel light and therefore speedily, covering an average of 12 to 15 miles a day and living off the land instead of relying on slow supply wagons or on depots requiring careful advance preparation. The army on the march was, thus, well spread out and extremely mobile, easily able to move into a loose net-like formation to trap enemy forces manoeuvring in a traditional compact group. They could then be rounded up, and forced to fight at a disadvantage. Campaigning for Napoleon was, until 1807, a successful blend of mobility, speed and surprise, which brought rich rewards. Not until the enemy learnt how to counter his strategies did the situation change.

Like all Revolutionary generals Napoleon was committed to the idea of the offensive and to the importance of forcing the enemy to give battle, but only when that enemy had been out-manoeuvred. While he was able to maintain the surprise element Napoleon won every encounter. At Ulm in 1805 the Austrians, remaining stationary, were surrounded. At the twin battles of Jena-Auerstädt in 1806 the Prussians, on the move, were surrounded and, worse still, found themselves facing the wrong way as the French attacked and the battle began. It was a textbook example of the inability of an old-fashioned army to meet Napoleon on equal terms. The Prussians, still operating in accordance with the teachings of Frederick the Great (most of their generals had learnt their craft in his campaigns), were organised in slow and unwieldy line-formation. Restricted in their movement, they were annihilated, losing 45,000 men and all their artillery.

While Napoleon's army remained a national one – the French nation in arms – fighting offensive wars and pursuing a policy of mobility and surprise against the old-fashioned, semi-static armies of the *ancien régime*, Clausewitz was right: Napoleon could not lose. In fact, so successful was he in his early campaigns that by his victories he changed the pattern of war. Instead of taking land in the eighteenth-century manner from states in decline (as Poland had been partitioned by her neighbours shortly before the Revolution) he took – and kept – territory belonging to the strong. His victories were so total that diplomats were not required for peace negotiations – he could, and did, dictate his own terms on the defeated. From 1805 onwards he developed the use of war as *une bonne affaire* (a good thing) financially. Peace treaties imposed on defeated countries not only provided for the free quartering of Napoleon's troops on their territory, but included the payment of massive indemnities – Prussia was forced to find 311 million francs after her defeat at Jena in 1806. War had become satisfactorily self-financing. It would continue to be so for Napoleon, as long as he went on winning.

e) Weapons and Training in the Grande Armée

Armies and their deployment might have changed, but the solders' weapons did not begin to do so until the middle of the nineteenth century, when industrial technology caught up with military theory. All Napoleon's campaigns were conducted using the weapons of the *ancien régime*. The musket was still the standard infantry weapon – a smooth-bored, muzzle-loading flintlock firing lead bullets, and fitted with a bayonet. Its fire power was limited, its rate of fire slow and its accuracy poor except at close range. The artillery was equally inaccurate and slow, with a range of about half a mile. It took a skilled gun crew to be able to fire a round a minute, even with the new, lighter cannon introduced into France in the 1770s. The use of horse artillery giving greater mobility to the guns, and the new practice of concentrating artillery fire in a barrage to open up gaps in the enemy's front line for infantry or cavalry to attack, were tactics of which Napoleon made good use, especially after 1806 as armies grew larger. They were not, however, his innovations – he had learnt them during his training as a young artillery cadet.

In some ways Napoleon was surprisingly conservative in his military thinking and could be unreceptive to developments in weaponry and military technology. He ignored new inventions brought to his attention, such as 'a water waggon driven by fire' (submarine), 'rockets' (incendiaires), the telegraph (a mechanical semaphore system), and the percussion charge (a replacement for the flint-lock). He seems to have known about but to have ignored also the cheap Prussian innovation of a sharp knife attached to a musket that could be used by the infantry to open the cartridges without having to waste time biting them, and so be able to fire more rapidly. He disbanded as unnecessary the small corps of (ground-anchored) observation balloons used for reconnaissance; but he reintroduced, for use by the heavy cavalry, the helmet and breastplate, already obsolete in the time of Louis XIV.

Training, for new recruits was very basic and continued to follow the programme, intended to combine enthusiasm with discipline, laid down for the Revolutionary armies in the early 1790s. A week in the home base was followed by a hardening-off march of 50 or 60 days to the front, practising drill and gaining experience by example along the way. Most practical training was still provided, especially in battle, by veteran soldiers in the tradition of the *amalgame* of 1793. In 1805, for instance, half the total strength of the army had fought under Napoleon at Marengo (1800), and a quarter had served in the Revolutionary wars; most of the officers and non-commissioned officers were experienced campaigners, although a high proportion of the ordinary soldiers were raw conscripts. The army consisted, therefore, of a mixture of old and young, experience and inexperience, combined under one command.

The size of Napoleon's *Grande Armée* (a name that he coined while with the army at Boulogne in 1805) has been disputed at length by military historians. For the years before 1805 estimates vary from about 300,000 upwards. It is now thought, based on the known average figure of 73,000 men enrolled each year in France, that in 1805–6 Napoleon's standing army numbered between 500,000 and 600,000. In addition he had other troops to call on, the auxiliary levies provided by the satellite states, which by 1807 represented about a third of the total strength of his armed forces.

f) Napoleon's Strategic Planning

It used to be stated in campaign histories that Napoleon planned his campaigns and battles well ahead and in meticulous detail, and that his victories came from following his plans minutely; but military historians are now much less certain that this was so. There is some evidence on this point from Napoleon himself, when, in 1804 and in rather boastful vein, he declared:

> Military science consists in calculating all the chances accurately in the first place and then giving accident, almost mathematically, its place in one's calculations. It is upon this point that one must not deceive oneself and that a fraction more or less may change everything. Now the apportioning of accident and science cannot get into any head, except that of a genius ... Accident, luck, chance, whatever you choose to call it – a mystery to ordinary minds – becomes a reality to superior minds.

A couple of years later he wrote to his brother Joseph that 'in war nothing is achieved except by calculation. Everything that is not soundly planned in its detail yields no result'.

Recent reassessments of Napoleon's military career suggest that while he always formulated a general plan, whether for a whole campaign or a particular battle – 'my great talent, the one that distinguishes me the most, is to see the *whole* picture distinctly' – he was basically an opportunist, prepared to adjust his plans according to changing circumstances and to take advantage of enemy errors or weakness. He could improvise brilliantly in the heat of battle and frequently did so, abandoning his original plan without hesitation. He was, however, always unwilling to take others into his confidence. This habit of keeping his ideas to himself resulted in a weakness of the command structure, which was to have serious results in later years.

In the same way, the old idea that Napoleon was forever moving his troops from one place to another, making in the process lightning marches across Europe, has been discredited. Such marches, like the famous one from the Channel coast to the Danube in 1805, were the exception. When he needed to Napoleon could organise the rapid movement of large numbers of men over wide areas to converge on his chosen target, but normally his marches were shorter, slower and less dramatic.

Whether he had 'a grand strategy' in the sense of a broad, overall design is difficult to say. The only consistent theme running through the years from 1800 to 1815 is enmity for Britain. Following the defeat of his invasion plan at Trafalgar in 1805, Napoleon did adopt another strategy to try to defeat Britain. His alternative plan was to turn the weapon of its own industrial and commercial superiority against Britain by attempting to destabilise the British economy. He therefore concentrated from 1805 onwards on dealing with his enemies on land, while keeping up an attack on Britain by means of the Continental System. This system envisaged blockading British trade by denying it access to European markets. The Continental System had an important consequence for the war since it meant the need for further conquests to try to close mainland Europe to British exports.

g) Napoleon's Generalship – An Assessment

Many historians are no longer ready to accept unquestioningly that Napoleon was a great general. R.S. Alexander believes that: 'His record was far from uniformly brilliant; it was marred by major defeats.'[6] They point out that he was in no way an innovator. He made no significant contribution to tactics, introduced no new weapons and was not open to new ideas. His contributions to strategy were not original. The armies he commanded were taken over from the Revolution, the *levée en masse* being established before he came to power. He introduced no new training methods. He underestimated supply problems, and made other errors of judgement, often because of his amazing, but unacknowledged, ignorance of climatic and geographical conditions. This led to avoidable losses in Egypt and in San Dominigue from heat and fever, from cold, snow, and mud on other occasions, the crossing of the Oder in 1806 for instance. Sometimes out of sheer obstinacy, as at Boulogne in 1805, he refused advice from those who knew better than to underestimate as he did the dangers to his ships from tide and weather. His lack of interest in the provision of maps covering the terrain over which he was to march, his often inadequate reconnaissance, and his failure to appreciate the difference between foraging in the prosperous and well-populated west of Europe and in the bare lands further east caused his men unnecessary hardship, as did his reduction of the army medical services to save money. He may have declared that the men's health was of paramount importance to him, but the sick and wounded on campaign were left to die.

Despite these well-founded criticisms, however, Napoleon was nevertheless a great general who achieved great conquests in a relatively short space of time. According to Charles Esdaille, a key factor in the dramatic improvement of French military fortunes after 1800 was 'the irreplaceable genius of Napoleon himself'.[7] Wellington thought that he was 'a great *homme de guerre*, possibly the greatest who ever appeared at the head of a French army'. Furthermore, Napoleon was not merely an inspired military leader: he also knew how to exploit his victories, to extract the maximum advantage from those he defeated. French domination therefore relied on diplomatic success as well as military achievements, and the great achievement of French diplomacy was to keep the coalition powers divided.[8]

His military reputation rests largely on the successes of his early campaigns in Italy and Egypt, and on those of 1805–6, when he was still young and energetic, full of enthusiasm and, it seemed, invincible. His methods, if not exactly new in theory, were new in practice and he used them well. They were a break with eighteenth-century tradition, and confusing to the opposition. Given his hold over his men and the incapacity of his enemies to match him and his army, his victories multiplied rapidly. If his career had finished in, say, 1807, it would have been one of undisputed military glory, justifying his admirers' plaudits. But it did not finish then, and the failures and defeats of the later years, the blunders and ill-judged decisions of the later campaigns, in Spain, in Russia, even at Waterloo, must be taken into account in painting the overall picture of Napoleon as a military leader.

h) The Weakness of Napoleon's Enemies – Allied Disunity

Britain, Russia, Austria and later Prussia formed a series of anti-French alliances with each other, but these were continually undermined by their mutual suspicions and jealousy. Only Britain remained opposed to France for the whole period. The other three powers were tempted away from time to time by Napoleon's offers of territory, for as well as making use of the opportunity to profit from quarrels among the allies, Napoleon's foreign policy was based on 'divide and rule'. His normal strategy was to keep at least one of these major powers as an ally while he dealt with the others.

i) The Second Coalition 1799

In the spring of 1799 the Second Coalition of Britain, Russia, Austria and the Ottoman Empire was at war with France. Theoretically a strong combination, it was in fact nothing of the sort. It was not an overall coalition, but a series of separate alliances, and even these links were not complete for there was no alliance between Britain and Austria. Even more important, there was no agreement on a unified military strategy, nor was there a commitment by the allies not to make a separate peace with France if it suited their interests to do so. Although Austrian and Russian forces pushed the French out of Italy in the summer of 1799 (this was part of the news that brought Napoleon hurrying back from Egypt and precipitated the *coup d'état* of Brumaire), an Anglo-Russian landing in Holland was unsuccessful and led to recriminations between the British and Russian commanders over whose fault it was that they had been defeated.

Relations between the two countries worsened over the question of control over French-held Malta, at that time being blockaded by Britain but promised by her to Russia in due course. At the same time a rift developed between Austria and the other two powers over Austrian suspicions of British intentions in Belgium and Russian ambitions in Italy. These differences exposed the much deeper divisions among the allies on the whole nature of the war against France. Russia was unsympathetic to the British view that the fight was one to destroy the Revolution totally, while Austria favoured the eighteenth-century view of the conflict as a limited one that would end in an exchange of territory – perhaps Belgium for Sardinia. The defeat of the Russian army by the French near Zurich in September 1799 led to the break-up of the Coalition, from which the Tsar withdrew in November of that year.

Over the winter of 1799–1800 Napoleon, now *First Consul*, tried with some success to win Tsar Paul over to his side, while also attempting to make peace with Austria and Britain. As the two allies could not agree between themselves what would be an equitable settlement, it proved impossible to reach an agreement. As a result, Napoleon decided that if France was to have peace he would have to impose it, but to do this he would have to defeat one of the allies first. Therefore he embarked on a second Italian campaign aimed against Austria, and forced her to accept the humiliating loss of all her Italian possessions, except Venice, at the Peace of Lunéville (February 1801). Meanwhile, Tsar Paul, irritated by Britain's refusal to give up Malta and by her high-handed behaviour over the interpretation of some aspects of maritime law, had formed a League of Armed Neutrality (Russia, Sweden, Denmark and Prussia) to keep Britain out of the Baltic. Although the assassination of the Tsar in March 1801 and Nelson's bombardment of Copenhagen the following month brought the League to a speedy end, the new Tsar, Alexander I, despite his anti-French sympathies, showed no signs of wishing to form an Anglo-Russian alliance. Isolated and tired of war, Britain had little choice but to accept the Peace of Amiens in March 1802.

ii) The Third Coalition 1805

In May 1803, after six months of deteriorating international relations, Britain declared war on France. However, there was little that Britain, with a strong navy but a very small army, could do on her own. In 1804 William Pitt, who had been Prime Minister since the resumption of hostilities, began the search for allies to join a Third Coalition. He announced his willingness to pay subsidies on an unprecedented scale to any ally willing to provide the troops needed to fight Napoleon on the continent, but neither Russia, Austria nor Prussia came forward. Austria and Russia were both anxious to see Napoleon defeated, but were not prepared to work together, for each still blamed the other for deserting the Second Coalition in 1799. In addition, Russia was not prepared to co-operate with Britain because the question of Malta was still unresolved.

References

1 T.C.W. Blanning, *The Origins of the French Revolutionary Wars* (Longman, 1986) p. 179.
2 François Furet, *The French Revolution 1770–1814* (Blackwell, 1996) p. 254
3 C. von Clausewitz, *On War* (Penguin, 1968) pp. 382–85
4 See Neil Stewart, *The Changing nature of Warfare* (Hodder and Stoughton, 2001) pp. 26–7.
5 Michael Howard, *War in European History* (OUP, 1976) p. 83.
6 R.S. Alexander, *Napoleon* (Arnold, 2001) p. 66.
7 C.J. Esdaille, *The Wars of Napoleon* (London, 1995), pp. 40–70.
8 Martyn Lyons, *Napoleon Bonaparte and the Legacy of the French Revolution* (Macmillan, 1994) pp. 196–7.

Summary Diagram
Napoleon and Europe: Conquest

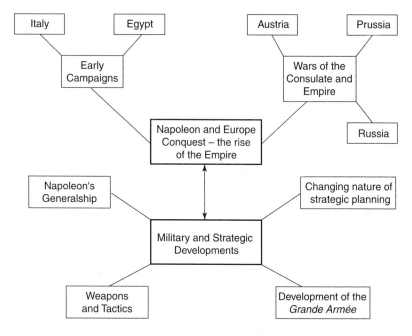

This chapter has considered an entirely different aspect of Napoleon's rule, namely his foreign policy. As a significant part of your course may consist of Napoleon and Europe, it is important that you pay very close attention to the content of this chapter. Note carefully his early campaigns and the extent to which these indicate any features that later appeared during his wars of conquests. To start with, it would be useful to identify each campaign and note its essential features – duration, location, opponent, outcome, special features etc. Try to provide as much relevant detail as possible. Remember to be concise in your note making, do not try and produce lengthy extracts of narrative. These notes if they are done well will provide you with a useful revision aid when you revisit this topic as part of your exam preparation.

Answering structured and essay questions on Chapter 5

In this chapter you have studied Napoleon's military and foreign policy, which had such major impact on the history of Europe. You have been presented with a range of new terminology and concepts. In preparing to answer structured and essay questions on this topic it is important that you are aware of the extent of your own knowledge and the particular demands of each question. While some of the questions may be directed at very specific areas of content, others will be much broader in their coverage. Ensure that you have both the necessary depth and breadth in terms of analytical and evaluative skills to answer any question you are given. Questions on this chapter fall neatly into one of two areas, namely the early campaigns, which were so successful, and the nature of warfare under Napoleon. While essay questions may retain this division it is possible that structured questions may combine aspects of both. Look at the following examples of structured questions:

1 **a)** Explain two main reasons why Napoleon was successful in his early campaigns. *(10 marks)*

   b) To what extent did Napoleon change the nature of warfare between 1796 and 1807? *(20 marks)*

2 **a)** Explain two military developments introduced by Napoleon. *(10 marks)*

   b) 'Napoleon was only successful in his early campaigns because his opponents were weak'. How far do you agree with this assessment of Napoleon's abilities as a commander? *(20 marks)*

Both questions **1a** and **b** will require you to provide specific content relating to Napoleon's early campaigns and his ability/skill as a general. Ensure that you try to give equal coverage to each part and remember that for each, factual content – dates, specific measures, place names and so on – will be well rewarded as long as it is accurate and relevant. Question **1b** will require you to focus on Napoleon's strategic and organisational abilities as well as technical innovations that were made. In Question **2a** choose any two military developments made by Napoleon, such as dividing the army into corps, and explain them fully. Question **2b** is more demanding in its scope since it will require you to assess why Napoleon was successful as a commander against a given view. Consider fully whether his opponent were weak before assessing Napoleon's own qualities as a commander.

Typical essay questions include the following;

1 'Napoleon's early victories in Italy suggested clearly the methods he would develop later'. How valid is this view of Napoleon's early campaigns?

2 'Qualities of leadership were far more important than weaknesses among his opponents'. To what extent is this a good evaluation of why Napoleon was so successful between 1796 and 1807?

3 'Napoleon changed the nature of warfare.' Discuss

Before attempting an essay under examination conditions you may wish to spend a few moments composing a rough plan of what it is you intend to cover. As long as the plan is not too detailed and does not take up too much of your precious examination, time this is good practice. Just simply jot down key phrases and points that you will want to address. You might also want to identify the key battles, treaties and military figures an examiner will expect to see included in any response. Remember to address the question and even include part of the question in your answer to emphasise that you are tackling the issue.

Answering Source-based questions on Chapter 5

1. Napoleon as a military commander
Study the two sources on pages 84 and 90 and answer the following questions:

a) Explain briefly the meaning of the following phrases – 'baton in his hand' (page 84, line 6), and 'military science' (page 90, line 1). (*6 marks*)

b) What does the source about the retreat from Moscow tell us about how Napoleon was viewed by the imperial army? (*10 marks*)

c) To what extent do both sources provide an insight into the qualities of leadership that Napoleon possessed? (*15 marks*)

6 Napoleon and Europe: Consolidation 1804–10

POINTS TO CONSIDER

This chapter covers the attempt by Napoleon to consolidate his conquests into the largest empire in Europe since Roman times. His approach to managing this vast empire was varied and, as you read the chapter for the first time, note how he proposed governing the various parts. Ask yourself whether they were treated equally or differently. You should also carefully consider what was Napoleon's motive in creating this vast structure. What did he hope to gain from it? Pay particular attention to the effects the creation of the empire had on the various peoples brought under French rule. One of the most important political forces to influence the course of the nineteenth century was nationalism. To what extent did Napoleon contribute to its development in the various territories he controlled.

KEY DATES

1804	18 May	Proclamation of Napoleon as Hereditary emperor of the French
1805		Annexation of the Ligurian Republic
		Creation of the Kingdom of Italy
1806		Kingdom of Holland created
	12 July	Confederation of the Rhine under Napoleon's protection
		Holy Roman Empire abolished
	21 November	Berlin Decree establishing Continental System
1807	19 July	Grand Duchy of Warsaw created
	8 August	Kingdom of Westphalia created
	25 October	Secret treaty between Napoleon and Spain to divide Portugal
	30 November	Lisbon occupied by General Junot
	17 December	Milan Decree to strengthen Continental System
1808	10 May	Spanish monarchy deposed, crown give to Joseph Bonaparte
	August	British troops land in Portugal
1809	Spring	Austria joins Britain in war against Napoleon
	14 October	Austria signs Peace of Vienna, Illyria ceded to Napoleon
1810		Bernadotte appointed crown Prince of Sweden and heir to the throne
	9 July	Holland annexed
	31 December	Tsar Alexander breaks Continental blockade by authorising trade with Britain

1 Establishing the Napoleonic Empire

KEY ISSUE What were the various parts that made up the Napoleonic Empire?

The Empire had its official birth on 18 May 1804, with the proclamation of Napoleon as hereditary Emperor of the French. The religious blessing of the empire occurred six months later with Napoleon's coronation at Notre Dame in the presence of the Pope. Its unofficial life, though, had begun long before 1804, with the Revolutionary conquests and those of the Consulate (see pages 78–81). Both of these had pushed the frontiers of 'old France' (the France of 1790) out towards her 'natural frontiers' – and beyond. The momentum of outward expansion followed closely the pace of military conquest.

The 'Empire' is often referred to as if it were a single entity embracing all French-controlled Europe. It was a more complicated arrangement than that. The French Empire, properly speaking, was France of the natural frontiers (Rhine, Alps, Pyrenees) plus the annexed territories (*pays réunis,* ruled from Paris) of Piedmont, Parma, Tuscany, the Papal States, the Illyrian Provinces and, after 1810, Holland. A semicircle of nominally independent satellite states (*pays conquis*) ruled by Frenchmen, usually Bonaparte relatives, formed a buffer zone protecting the borders of the French Empire from attack. These states, combined with the French Empire proper, formed the Grand Empire. In the west, the satellites included at various times Switzerland, the kingdoms of Spain, Naples, and Italy; Napoleon's Germanic Confederation of the Rhine (of which the kingdom of Westphalia formed part); and, until 1810, Holland. In eastern Europe there was the Grand Duchy of Warsaw that had been created out of the conquered Polish lands as a barrier to Russian expansion into central Europe. (See page 99 for a reference list of the Imperial Territories, and also the map on page 119.)

There were also a small group of allied states (*pays alliés*) in the Confederation of the Rhine that were ruled by their native sovereigns but owed allegiance to Napoleon. Included in these states was Saxony, whose king was given oversight of the Grand Duchy of Warsaw by Napoleon. Of the great powers, Austria, Prussia and Russia were each from time to time brought by military or diplomatic pressures into Napoleon's direct sphere of influence and each in turn became his ally, though not always willingly and only for a limited period. Even the outlying Baltic powers came within Napoleon's orbit when he involved them in operating the Continental Blockade – Sweden, much weakened by the loss of Finland to Russia as the result of an attack instigated by France, fared particularly badly and had in 1810 to accept a Napoleonic marshal as heir to the Swedish throne. In Europe only the Ottoman Empire and Britain remained always outside Napoleon's control.

Territories of the Empire – A Reference List

Revolutionary Period 1790–9

1790   'Old France', 83 departments, 28 million inhabitants
1791   23 military divisions created

Territories Annexed:
1791   Avignon
1792   Savoy
1793   Nice
1795   Belgium and Luxemburg
1798   German left bank of the Rhine

'Sister Republics' Created:
1795   Batavian Republic (Holland)
1797   Cisalpine Republic (North Italy) became Republic of Italy 1801
1797   Ligurian Republic (Genoa)
1798   Helvetic Republic (Switzerland)

Consulate Period 1799–1804

1800   France (including Belgium), 98 departments, 33 million inhabitants

Territories Annexed:
1802   Piedmont (conquered 1796–7) now formally annexed
1803   Swiss Confederation reorganised with Napoleon as 'Mediator'

The Empire Period 1804–14

1804   108 departments

Territories Annexed:
1805   Ligurian Republic
1808   Parma and Kingdom of Etruria (Grand Duchy of Tuscany created for Napoleon's sister Elise 1809)
1809   Papal States (the part not already included 1808 in satellite Kingdom of Italy). Rome named 'second city of Empire', 1810
1809   Illyrian Provinces
1810   Kingdom of Holland annexed (Napoleon considered Louis to be too lenient with the Dutch to remain king of a satellite Holland)
1811   The Hansa towns of Hamburg, Bremen and Lübeck, and Duchy of Oldenburg

Satellite states created:

1805 Kingdom of Italy created out of Republic of Italy with Napoleon as king, but ruled by Eugène de Beauharnais, Napoleon's stepson, as viceroy

1806 Venetia incorporated into Kingdom of Italy

1806 Kingdom of Naples created with Napoleon's brother Joseph as king

1806 Kingdom of Holland created out of Batavian Republic with Napoleon's brother Louis as king (until annexed in 1810)

1806 Confederation of the Rhine formed with Napoleon as 'Protector'. Holy Roman Empire abolished. The Confederation initially had 16 member states – later others were incorporated included the kingdoms of Saxony and Westphalia

1807 Kingdom of Westphalia created, partly from Prussian and Hanoverian territory, with Napoleon's brother Jérôme as king

1807 Portugal subjugated; French general appointed governor 1808

1807 Grand Duchy of Warsaw created out of the conquered Polish lands and given to the king of Saxony to administer

1808 Kingdom of Spain created and Napoleon's brother Joseph moved from Naples to be king. Joachim Murat, husband of Napoleon's sister, Caroline, made king of Naples

1808 Papal States (part) incorporated into Kingdom of Italy

1809 Trentino and South Tyrol incorporated into Kingdom of Italy

1810 Remainder of Hanover (occupied by French since 1804) ceded to Kingdom of Westphalia, although the best lands were detached and given to Napoleon's *Domaine extraordinaire*

1810 French influence extended into the Baltic by the appointment of the Napoleonic marshal Bernadotte as Crown Prince of Sweden and heir to the throne, and by Scandinavian involvement in the Continental Blockade

1811 Napoleon's European territories reached their greatest extent:

The French Empire (i.e. France of the natural frontiers plus the annexed territories) contained 130 departments, 44 million inhabitants, 32 military divisions

The Grand Empire (i.e. the French Empire plus the satellite states) contained over 80 million inhabitants.

2 Consolidating the Empire

> **KEY ISSUES** What methods did Napoleon use to control the
> Empire? What did he hope to provide for his subjects?

The states of the Grand Empire fell into one of two categories – lands
annexed directly to France, or satellite states under French control
but notionally enjoying a measure of independence. Treatment
varied according to which category a state was in. The extent of
Napoleonic influence varied too, depending on the length of time a
particular country remained under his authority. The greatest impact
was felt in those annexed regions that were closest to France itself and
that were subject to her laws and influence the longest.

a) The Annexed Territories

Among the annexed territories, Nice, Savoy, Belgium and the
German lands west of the Rhine were under French control for the
greatest period of time. They had been annexed before 1799, and
had been quickly incorporated into the French administrative system,
being divided into departments for civil affairs and into military divisions for recruiting purposes. By the time of Brumaire, feudalism had
been abolished in these territories as it had been in France. Feudal
dues were done away with, and property and lands belonging to the
nobility or church were confiscated and sold. In 1802 Piedmont,
under French occupation since 1796, was formally annexed, as was
the Ligurian Republic in 1805. Ruled from Paris, all these states came
to be regarded as territorial extensions of the 'old France', and an
integral part of the new Napoleonic France. All the national institutions flourished there: the Concordat and the Civil Code, the
Imperial University, the judicial process of civil and criminal courts.
There was rather less welcome for the imposition of the taxation
system and the liability for conscription.

Research on conditions in these annexed territories has concentrated not so much on legal, economic and administrative changes
brought about there, as on looking at the evidence for an underlying
social and economic continuity from pre- to post-Napoleonic times.
In Piedmont, where the feudal system was in decline before the
French conquests of 1796–7 and freehold property was already a
common form of land tenure, it is now thought that the introduction
of French law brought little novelty and simply gave legal recognition
to an existing situation. In the economically developed lands on the
west bank of the Rhine the bourgeoisie adapted to the new methods,
while at the same time retaining old ones. They fell in first with the
wishes of their French rulers and after 1815 with those of their new
masters, the Prussians, while managing at the same time to defend

and maintain their pre-Napoleonic social status along with their old trade privileges, traditional local customs and commercial interests.

German and Italian territories that were annexed in 1806–9 (see Reference List on page 99) were subject to French law and influence for a much shorter time. As a result they do not appear to have had any profound or long-lasting effects from the changes introduced by Napoleon. Indeed there is some suggestion that in these territories their social structure did not change much from that of the old régimes.

b) The Satellite States

The satellite states, although nominally independent, in fact had little freedom of action. From the beginning their rulers were strictly supervised and tutored by Napoleon in the way they should go:

Napoleon's stepson, Eugène de Beauharnais was told:

> By entrusting you with the government of Our Kingdom of Italy we have given you proof of the respect which your conduct has inspired in Us. But you are still at an age [23] when one does not realise the perversity of men's hearts: I cannot therefore recommend too strongly caution and watchfulness ... let no one have your complete confidence and never tell anyone what you think ... If you ever find yourself speaking ... from the heart, say to yourself 'I have made a mistake' and don't do it again. The less you talk the better ... learn to listen and remember that silence is often as effective as a display of knowledge: however much people flatter you, they all know your limitations ... So long as a prince holds his tongue, his power is incalculable.

When the new Kingdom of Westphalia was established in 1807, Napoleon in a letter to his brother Jérôme suggested some approaches to governing his new subjects and the benefits of French rule:

Napoleon on the benefits of French rule

Fontainebleau, 15 November 1807

To Jérôme Bonaparte, King of Westphalia

My Dear brother, You will find enclosed the constitution of your kingdom... You must observe it faithfully ... They are more enlightened in the Kingdom of Westphalia than some would have you believe; and your throne will only become truly established with the confidence and the affection of the people. What the peoples of Germany impatiently desire is that men of talent, who lack noble rank, will have an equal claim to your favour and to government employment; they also demand that all kinds of servitude be entirely abolished... The benefits of the *Code Napoléon*, public trials, the introduction of juries, will be distinctive features of your rule ... It is necessary for your subjects to enjoy a degree of liberty, equality and prosperity hitherto unknown among the peoples of Germany; and that your liberal government produces, one way or another, changes which will be most beneficial to the Confederation of the Rhine and the strength of your monarchy. Such a method of government will prove a more powerful barrier separating you from Prussia than the Elbe, the fortresses and the protection of France. What people would wish to return to the arbitrary government of Prussia when they have tasted the benefits of wise and liberal administration? The peoples of Germany, as well as those of France, Italy and Spain, desire equality and demand liberal ideas ... Be a constitutional king.

On many occasions Napoleon wrote to his brothers setting out his fervent desire for the well-being of the imperial subjects, for example – 'The aim of your administration is the happiness of My Italian peoples ... count yourself a failure unless the Italians believe you love them'; but this was mere window-dressing. Napoleon was not concerned with fostering the simple happiness of the common people, nor, despite his assertions, with encouraging the spread of liberty and equality by actively ending feudalism throughout the Empire. It would appear that feudalism was abolished more in legal principle than in actuality in the satellite states, and that it survived in many areas in its old form of noble privileges, feudal dues, serfdom and even labour services.

This would suggests that the traditional view that Napoleon abolished feudalism in the territories he conquered needs to be modified. At best his achievements in this direction seem to have been patchy and largely restricted to the countries annexed early. Continental research on the subject indicates that part of Napoleon's reforms remained more theoretical than actual, and that he in effect settled for a pragmatic compromise with the traditional feudal structures of the satellite states. It now seems likely that pre-Napoleonic noble or bourgeois élitist groups continued to survive in sufficient numbers for the social structure to remain largely unchanged in much of Italy, Germany and Poland. This, it can be argued, was one reason why the Empire collapsed so quickly in 1814, and why the allies met with little opposition in restoring the old dynasties and régimes at the Vienna Congress – a suitable social infrastructure was already in place in the countries concerned.

3 Why was the Empire Created?

KEY ISSUES What are the various explanations behind why the Empire was created? Did Napoleon promote nationalism?

Napoleon's own explanation for the need to expand his territories was:

- to protect the territory of Revolutionary France from attack by the 'old monarchies' of Europe
- to export the Civil Code, the Concordat and other benefits of Napoleonic rule to the oppressed peoples of neighbouring states
- to provide oppressed peoples with liberty, equality and prosperity
- to ensure the end of the old regimes in Europe
- to provide guarantees to citizens everywhere in the Empire against arbitrary government action.

These praiseworthy aims were the public face of imperial expansion – less noble sentiments were expressed more truthfully in private by Napoleon. To the kings of the satellite states he wrote that they must establish the Civil Code because 'it will fortify your power, since by it all entails are cancelled and there will no longer be any great estates except those you create yourselves. This is the motive which has led me to recommend a civil code and its establishment everywhere'.

Historians have argued at length over what really drove Napoleon to create the Empire. Geoffrey Ellis believes that Napoleon's conquests offered him opportunities to exploit the territories not only to secure his military domination but also to reorganise the civil life of the annexed lands. His imperial vision became a natural extension of his personal dynastic ambition. Napoleon believed that 'what was good for Napoleon must be good for France, and so in turn good for the conquered Europe as a whole.'[1]

As so often in dealing with Napoleon, the situation is confused. It is difficult to determine from the evidence available, much of which is contradictory, which of his words and deeds were preplanned and which were spontaneous; which reflected his real policies and which were pragmatic compromises. As he himself said, 'I would often have been hard put to it to be able to assert with any degree of truth what was my whole and real intention'. It is probable that no single interpretation provides a complete answer to the question of Napoleon's motives. In the past, overweening ambition, personal glory, and the pursuit of power for its own sake were generally considered his guiding principles, but these now seem rather simplistic explanations for such a complex personality. There may well have been other motives as well, forming a much more diverse pattern than was previously thought, with different elements predominating at different times. One of these elements was undoubtedly his preoccupation with the idea of a universal empire. Another, and less credible, one was his alleged desire to encourage nationalism in the countries of the Empire.

a) Universal Empire

In 1812 one of his advisers dared mention to Napoleon that 'the Great Powers are becoming afraid of a universal monarchy. Your dynasty is already spreading everywhere, and other dynasties fear to see it established in their own countries'. However, Napoleon was not annoyed but pleased with the information. A universal monarchy was the first step towards achieving his long-held dream of a universal empire made up of French-controlled vassal states. Metternich, the Austrian Chancellor, certainly thought this dream was the basis of Napoleon's ambition:

Napoleon's system of conquests was unique. The object of universal domination to which he aspired was not the concentration of an enormous region in the immediate hands of the government, but the establishing of a central supremacy over the states of Europe, after the ideal of the Empire of Charlemagne.

Support for Metternich's belief can be found in Napoleon's quite extraordinary correspondence with the Pope between 1806 and 1808 that reveals his obsession with Charlemagne. The Holy Roman Emperor (one of the titles of the Austrian Emperor), still widely regarded as Charlemagne's titular successor, had been dispossessed by Napoleon, who, at least in his own mind, had taken his place when he crowned himself as King of Italy at Milan in May 1805:

As far as the Pope is concerned, I *am* Charlemagne. Like Charlemagne I join the crown of France with the iron crown of Lombardy, My Empire, like Charlemagne's marches with the east. I therefore expect the Pope to accommodate his conduct to my requirements. If he behaves well [i.e. implements the Continental Blockade] I shall make no outward changes – if not, I shall reduce him to the status of a Bishop of Rome.

By 1808, having failed to come to an agreement with the Pope, Napoleon took upon himself the right, as the new Charlemagne, to quash the Donation of his predecessor, imprison the Pope and annex the Papal States to the kingdom of Italy. (This Donation was the gift of Rome and most of Italy to the Pope, and was alleged to have been made by Charlemagne to provide temporal as well as spiritual power for the Church.)

At the height of his power (1811), Napoleon's Empire with its satellite, family-ruled kingdoms exceeded the limits of Charlemagne's; his son's title of King of Rome, formerly borne by the Habsburg heirs to the Holy Roman Empire, underlined his Imperial power and dynastic legitimacy. It is possible that it was at this point that Napoleon began to regard the Empire of Charlemagne as merely a first stage in his ambitions, and to look to founding a new Roman Empire as his future goal. This, given Napoleon's known admiration for Caesar (and Alexander) as well as Charlemagne, his interest in the East and his decision to make Rome the second city of his Empire, is a possibility, but no more, for there is no real evidence to substantiate the theory.

b) Nationalism

In the accounts that he dictated on St Helena, Napoleon spoke about the hopes he had entertained of fulfilling the national aspirations of his subject peoples and of his sorrow that the behaviour of the 'old monarchies' had prevented him from doing so. Given time and peace, he told Las Cases, on St Helena, he would have been successful in a programme of national unification:

> One of my grandest ideas was *l'agglomération*; the concentration of peoples geographically united, but separated by revolutions and political action. There are scattered over Europe more than 30 million French, 15 million Spanish, 15 million Italians and 30 million Germans. My intention was to make each of these peoples into a separate national state. As regards the 15 million Italians, *l'agglomération* had already gone far; it needed only time to mature; every day ripened that unity of principles and legislation, of thought and of feeling, which is the sure and infallible cement of human societies. The annexation of Piedmont and Parma were only temporary expedients; the single aim was to guide, guarantee and hasten the national education of the Italian people.

At one time these declarations were taken at their face value. Now they are considered as Napoleon's desire to liberalise his image (see pages 144–5) in the light of changing political circumstances after 1815. Whatever he may have said after 1815, while in power he never tolerated nationalist ambitions among his subject peoples – or their rulers. He became 'increasingly ruthless and despotic'[2] in his dealings with them, appearing in later years as the dictator who alone knew what was best for the Empire:

> … my Italian subjects know me too well to forget that there is more in my little finger than in all their heads put together. In Paris where people are more enlightened than in Italy, they hold their tongues and bow to the judgement of a man who has proved that he sees further and more clearly than they do. I am surprised that in Italy they are less obliging. (1806)
> I understand Italian affairs better than anyone else. (1810)

When, in 1810, Holland was annexed to France, Napoleon wrote:

> I shall do what suits the interests of My Empire. I did not take over the government of Holland in order to consult the common people of Amsterdam or to do what they want. The French nation has been wise enough to rely upon my judgement. My hope is that the Dutch will come to have the same opinion of me.

The Dutch, however, had a very different opinion of their new political masters. Charles Lebrun, the official appointed as Governor-General of the annexed Dutch territories, informed Napoleon in 1811:

> I told Your Majesty that tranquility reigns here. I did not say that there is general contentment ... I hope that the enemy will not appear, but should that happen I doubt very much that we could count on the help of the Dutch.

In Spain he so misjudged the situation that he expected to impose French rule there with little or no difficulty:

> Some agitations may take place, but the good lesson which has just been given the city of Madrid [the massacre carried out by Murat in May 1808] will naturally soon settle affairs ... The Spaniards are like other people and are not a class apart; they will be happy to accept the imperial institutions.

The belief that Napoleon was a reformer who consciously rationalised and systematised the conquered territories, socially, legally and economically, and so began the process of 'modernisation' in Germany and Italy, has now been revised. It remains true, however, that by 1811, geographically speaking, he had simplified the map of Europe by amalgamating and rearranging small states into larger blocks; but this was done without regard to national considerations. The new blocks were simply constructed as convenient administrative units for the Grand Empire.

Napoleon's universal Empire, by its very nature, ran counter to the principle of nationality. How was it, then, that Napoleon came to be so firmly associated with paving the way for national unity among the peoples of the Empire? That belief was based on Napoleon's own words about wanting to 'unify each of these peoples', words that are now viewed as no more than wishful thinking – part of his attempt to rewrite history. While he took no positive steps to encourage nationalism, in a negative way, however, the effect of his military actions and annexations *was* to arouse nationalist ambitions in Germany and, to a lesser extent, in Italy, Poland, Spain and Russia.

In the later eighteenth century, even before the French Revolution, philosophers were thinking seriously of nationalism as an important new force in contemporary politics: 'A kingdom consisting of a single nation is a family, a well-regulated household; it ... is founded by nature and stands and falls by time alone. An empire, formed by forcing together a hundred nations and a hundred and fifty provinces, is no body politic, but a monster', at least according to one late-eighteenth century German writer. The success of the Revolution in establishing, during the 1790s, a spirit of French unity and national solidarity encouraged nationalist murmurings elsewhere in Europe, where new importance was being attached to local customs and traditional culture, to shared national language and beliefs. Napoleonic imperialism gave a further impetus to nationalist developments by provoking a spirit of resistance to foreign, that is French, rule and to the military and financial burdens that accompanied it. Nowhere was this process more marked than in Germany, and most particularly in Prussia.

As the eighteenth century was drawing to a close Germany was enjoying a great cultural renaissance in which music, philosophy and literature all played a part. The playwright Schiller defined the current mood when he wrote in 1802, 'The greatness of Germany consists in its culture and the character of the nation, which are independent of its political fate'. The catastrophic defeat of Prussia in 1806 at the battle of Jena changed the whole situation. The process of Prussian recovery changed cultural self-satisfaction into political nationalism, which began with a strange mixture of adopting French ideas and reacting against French domination. Its development was unintentionally assisted by Napoleon when he defeated Austria and destroyed the Holy Roman Empire, weakening the political influence of the Habsburgs, which had always been a divisive one, and encouraging the Prussian ideas of leading a future united all-German state. With the dual aims of military reform and internal reorganisation, Prussia created a national army, and a strong central government, together with a new education system. All designed along French lines, they were intended to stimulate in the people a common spirit of patriotic devotion to the cause of *German* nationalism. 'I know only one Fatherland and that is Germany' said one of the chief Prussian reformers; and in 1813 the battle of Leipzig, which drove out the French and destroyed the Confederation of the Rhine, became a German patriotic legend.

In Italy the situation was different. There was none of the idea of a *Volk* there, a people bound together by a common heritage and shared language, as there was in Germany. Italian sentiment, too, was less generally anti-French than elsewhere. Indeed, the urban middle class actively welcomed the reduction of Catholic power brought about by Napoleon's confrontation with the Pope. There was little or no public response during the Hundred Days to the proclamation issued by the flamboyant Murat, Napoleon's brother-in-law and King of Naples, declaring war on Austria and calling on all Italians to fight for national unity and independence. (His campaign was initially successful when he marched north and captured Rome and Bologna, but soon afterwards he was defeated by an Austrian army, and was later shot.) The idea that Napoleon paved the way for Italian unification, and that his rule 'was a landmark in the history of the *Risorgimento*' (the Italian nineteenth-century nationalist movement) is only indirectly true. Italian national aspirations did not gain ground until *after* 1815, as a political reaction to the unwelcome restoration of most of the old ruling families and the old régimes.

Napoleon's part in the growth of Polish nationalism is a strange one. Between 1772 and 1795 Poland had been divided up between her neighbours, Russia, Austria and Prussia. It was given a new, if partial, lease of life by Napoleon, when he created the satellite Grand Duchy of Warsaw in 1807 and gave it a new constitution. This was welcomed by the Poles with enormous enthusiasm as a step towards the full reinstatement of their country. Napoleon, however, ignored Polish nationalist ambitions and used the Duchy simply as a source of military supplies and a pawn in his dealings with Russia. In 1812 when he needed troops for the Russian campaign, he made actual if vague promises of future independence for the Poles in return for 98,000 men. The men were found but the promises were never fulfilled. Nevertheless, the Poles continued to support Napoleon to the bitter end, and for their pains lost everything. Poland was again divided among her neighbours at Vienna; but Polish nationalism did not die. It survived, based on Romantic traditions of military glory gained by her soldiers as a part of Napoleon's *Grande Armée* on battlefields all over Europe. These heroics sustained the Poles well into the twentieth century, during which time Napoleon, who treated them so cynically, continued to appear in art and literature as the focus for their dreams of national independence.

Russia and Spain are usually included in the list of countries where Napoleon's activities are claimed to have had some influence on the development of nationalism. However, although in both countries the people were temporarily united by hatred of the French invaders and by the savagery of the fighting, any lasting effects were in fact minimal.

The whole question of Napoleon's relationship with nationalism is a complicated one. As a young man he had experienced and sympathised with the rise of nationalist sentiments in France during the Revolution. He spoke later about the 'great people' and their right to nationhood; but what was right for his own people was not in his opinion the automatic right of others. It was 'France first and always', and the Empire must serve the interests of France. Napoleon did not fully appreciate that sweeping away the old ruling dynasties of Europe and replacing them with an unwelcome foreign government would create, especially in Germany, the very thing he was trying to avoid, the growth of nationalist aspirations. Nationalism within the Empire was, though, largely the prerogative of the intellectual middle classes, and hardly touched the mass of the people, who had enough to do to keep themselves and their families alive without worrying about political ideas. It would be wrong, therefore, to consider the basically peasant armies of the Allies as fighting a war of 'national' liberation in 1813 as some historians have claimed. At the so-called 'Battle of the Nations' (Leipzig) they fought out of traditional loyalty to the *ancien régime* and to drive away the French, not for reasons of national pride.

4 Napoleon's Expectations from the Empire

> **KEY ISSUES** What did Napoleon want from his empire? Did the various territories of the empire benefit or suffer from French rule?

French military expenditure soared from 462 million francs in 1807 to 817 million francs in 1813. To a considerable degree Napoleon's imperialism was paid for by his defeated enemies. 'War, to put it bluntly, would support war'.[3] After Jena Prussia had to pay France 311 million francs, roughly equivalent to half the French government's ordinary revenue. Napoleon's expectations from the annexed territories and from the satellite states were, naturally enough, different. The annexed territories were treated as the rest of France. They enjoyed the same rights, and were subject to the same social and legal obligations, as well as the provision of conscripts and the payment of taxes.

The position of the satellite states was very different. They were never allowed to forget that they existed only to serve the interests of France. They not only formed a strategically important buffer zone to protect French borders, but fulfilled a number of other valuable functions in Napoleon's imperial enterprise. They were first and foremost military vassal states and Napoleon's relationship with them was eventually very like that of a medieval 'warrior overlord', extracting the maximum advantage from them for the minimum return. They raised about a third of the total strength of the *Grande Armée* in the form of auxiliary troops, and were used to support and provision the regular army that continued in the Revolutionary tradition to 'live off the land' wherever it was garrisoned outside France. In addition, as the price of defeat, they had to pay substantial tribute monies that were used to finance Napoleon's future campaigns.

A good example of Napoleon's treatment of a satellite state is the Kingdom of Italy. The military and financial demands made on it in the interests of France ruined its economy. From 1806 onwards its 6 million inhabitants had to pay an annual tribute of £1.5 million to the French treasury, as well as making substantial cash contributions for such enterprises as ship-building. When the supply of currency ran out and the Viceroy protested that it was impossible for the kingdom, now heavily in debt, to continue supporting 100,000 French troops on its soil or to find any more ready money, Napoleon replied not with help but by adding to its obligations the outstanding debts of the Papal States, and by demanding a year later an extra £1.5 million towards the cost of the campaign in Russia. The kingdom was also forced to recruit and maintain an army of 55,000 men for French service outside Italy. When conscription was introduced the effect on the population of Rome was dramatic. The population fell from 136,268 in 1809 to 112,648 in 1814 largely as a direct result of young men trying to avoid being called up.[4] In addition to all this, the working of the Continental Blockade placed a severe strain on the commercial life of the country and destroyed its silk industry. The story in other satellite states was not dissimilar.

As well as their military and financial uses, the satellite states provided for Napoleon's dynastic and social needs. The distribution of crowns among Bonaparte relatives served two purposes for Napoleon. It enabled him to fulfil his clan loyalties to his brothers and sisters, with the expectation that in return they would remain loyal to him and so secure his hold over the Empire. Also, with such a large number of Bonaparte sovereigns available, he could expect in due course to arrange useful marriage alliances with older royal houses and give his successors the dynastic respectability the family presently lacked.

When the Imperial nobility was created it became necessary to endow them with lands and revenues. The completeness of the Revolutionary land settlement left Napoleon with no suitable available land in France for these endowments, nor for rewarding lesser military or civilian personnel. The satellite states were used to provide the necessary land. Poland in particular was despoiled in this way, to the grave detriment of her economy. Even before the formal creation of the Grand Duchy of Warsaw, major endowments of land were made to 27 French marshals and generals. These gifts alone were on a scale that deprived the Duchy treasury of a fifth of its potential revenue from the former royal lands. The loss of income from further enormous land-gifts, added to other financial demands, ended by bankrupting the Duchy.

In a typical outburst Napoleon scolded his brother Louis, King of Holland, for not putting France first at all times:

> I myself drew up the constitution which was to provide the basis of your Majesty's throne on which I placed you. I hoped that developing in close proximity to France, Holland would possess that affection for France which the French nation has the right to expect of its children, and even more so of its princes. I hoped that, raised in my political principles, you would feel that Holland, which has been conquered by my subjects, only owes its independence to their generosity; that Holland lacking allies and an army could be, and would deserve to be, conquered on the day it sets itself in opposition to France ... I have sufficient grievances against Holland to declare war on her.

In 1806 he spelled out just as clearly to Joseph, the King of Naples, the need to give priority to French interests and to instil fear in order to govern effectively and maintain the stability of the Empire:

> I see that you promise in one of your proclamations not to impose any war taxation and that you forbid Our soldiers to demand full board from their hosts ... these measures are too narrowly conceived. You do not win people to your side by cajoling them ... Levy a contribution of 30 millions from the kingdom of Naples ... it would be ridiculous if the conquest of Naples did not bring comfort and well-being to My army ... If you do not make yourself feared from the beginning you are bound to get into trouble ... your proclamations do not make it clear enough who is master. You will gain nothing by too many caresses ... if they [the people] detect they have no master over them, they will turn to rebellion and mutiny.

In no context was the subservient position of the satellite states made more obvious than in connection with the operation of the Continental Blockade as a 'one-way common market'.

a) The Effect of the Continental Blockade on the Empire

Historians are divided in their views on whether the annexed lands benefited or not from Napoleon's control over their affairs. Michael Broers, for instance, considers that the experience of what he notes as the outer empire (Spain and the Illyrian provinces) was 'truly a short sharp shock'.[5] On the other hand some consider it to have brought valuable material advantages in its wake and, at least for a time, one of these advantages may well have been the working of the Continental Blockade, for part of its purpose was to protect home markets against foreign competition. Theoretically, home markets included those of the annexed territories. Industry in Belgium, such as textiles and manufacturing, generally benefited from access to the large Imperial domestic market. The experience of Piedmont, however, was very different. It was greatly discriminated against as was the Kingdom of Italy in the matter of exporting silk. In order to increase production by the silk manufacturers of Lyon, Piedmont was prohibited from providing silk for manufacture anywhere else. As far as the satellite states were concerned, the Blockade operated entirely to their disadvantage. Against them one-sided preferential tariffs and equally one-sided trade restrictions were imposed.

The Imperial decrees of 1806 and 1810, for instance, abolished the traditional trading links between the Kingdom of Italy and her neighbours. All export trade must be with France only; at the same time Italy was 'reserved' as a market, or rather 'dumping ground', for French goods of all kinds at high prices. Eugène de Beauharnais, Viceroy of the Kingdom of Italy, was threatened with annexation by Napoleon if his country exported silk anywhere except to France:

> It is no use for Italy to make plans that leave French prosperity out of account. Above all she must be careful not to give France any reason for annexing her; for if it paid France to do this, who could stop her? So make this your motto too: France first [*la France avant tout*].

Louis, King of Holland, received a warning about his slackness in enforcing the Blockade:

> ... the independence of Holland can continue only so long as it is not incompatible with the interests of France ... Unless care is taken to avoid thwarting the system of trade [the Continental Blockade] laid down by France, Holland may lose her independence.

Apart from the manufacturing industries, Napoleon's economic policy also had a blighting effect on farming communities in the satellite states, especially in the good years when France produced enough food of her own and there was nowhere else to which they were allowed to send their surplus foodstuffs. This resulted in severely depressed agricultural prices in much of the Empire, which in turn led to a lower standard of living for those who could no longer afford the inflated prices demanded for imported French goods, the only ones available for purchase.

b) Summary

Napoleon's Imperial policies were not altruistic. He had no intention of exporting the benefits of the Revolution to the rest of Europe, nor of fostering happiness among his peoples, nor of developing national unity in Germany, Italy or elsewhere. As Martin Lyons points out: 'Napoleon's priority was imperial conquest and not ideological subversion'.[6] These things might happen as the result of Imperial expansion, but if they did, they were purely incidental to it, not the mainspring for it.

Was Napoleon's Empire founded on unbounded personal ambition, desire for military glory, a dictator's hunger for power, or the patriot's ambition to see France secure, pre-eminent in Europe, and the ideas of the Revolution safeguarded – or some combination of these? Was he motivated by the dream of universal empire, or driven by the need to fulfil the destiny he believed in? The questions are open ones – the answers must depend, as always in dealing with Napoleon, on individual interpretation of the facts as far as they can be known, weighing up the probabilities and analysing the evidence. Much hinges on the complexities of Napoleon's own character and it might be helpful to reflect on what you have already covered before trying to decide what were the motives underlying the foundation of the Napoleonic Empire.

References

1 Geoffrey Ellis, *Napoleon* (Longman, 1997) p. 81.
2 Derek McKay and H.M. Scott, *The Rise of the Great Powers 1648–1815* (Longman, 1983) p. 321.
3 Paul Kennedy, *The Rise and Fall of the Great Powers* (Fontana, 1988) p. 172.
4 Michael Broers, *Europe under Napoleon 1799–1815* (Arnold, 1996) p. 207.
5 Michael Broers, *Europe under Napoleon 1799–1815* (Arnold, 1996) p. 202.
6 Martin Lyons, *Napoleon Bonaparte and the Legacy of the French Revolution* (Macmillan, 1994) p. 195.

Summary Diagram
Napoleon and Europe: Consolidation 1804–10

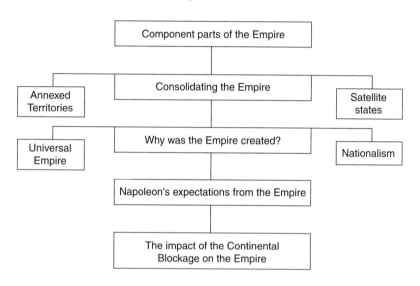

Working on Chapter 6

This important chapter looks at how the grand Empire was organised and how some in the occupied territories reacted to French rule. Pay close attention to what Napoleon expected from his empire and try to decide whether he achieved any of his requirements. As you read through this chapter, imagine how citizens in the occupied territories would have reacted to French rule, and also how soldiers in the French army might have viewed their service beyond the frontiers of France. Remember that a contemporary evaluation will very likely be influenced by the personal circumstances of the author of the source. After you have read the chapter, attempt a cost/benefit analysis of French rule in the Empire.

Answering structured and essay questions on Chapter 6

Now that you have been introduced to the concept of the Grand Empire and are starting to become familiar with its various component parts and structures. Try the following questions as part of your revision on the content of this chapter:

1 **a)** Explain carefully two methods by which Napoleon sought to control the Grand Empire. (*20 marks*)
  b) How successful was Napoleon in controlling the various territories that were brought under French rule? (*40 marks*)
2 **a)** Explain two aims of Napoleon's policy towards the Grand empire. (*20 marks*)
  b) How successful was France in exploiting the occupied territories? (*40 marks*)

The first part of each of the two questions is clear in its requirement. You need to provide two specific areas of content. Where possible give the examiner as much relevant detail as you can – names of places and individuals, dates of measures, battles and occupation. In the second part you will need to evaluate and consider arguments for and against the question. Balance your response and ensure that you reach a substantiated judgement, supported by relevant factual content.

In the essay questions the possible issues could range from how the French controlled their empire, the nature of French rule, through to Napoleon's thoughts in exile regarding his thwarted plans. Consider the following:

1 'The only people to benefit from French rule were the French'. How valid is this view of the Napoleonic Empire?
2 'Napoleon's priorities regarding the empire were conquest and exploitation'. How far do you agree with this view of French rule over Europe under Napoleon?
3 To what extent did the occupied territories benefit from French rule under Napoleon?
4 How successfully did Napoleon control the territories he occupied?

The first two essay questions require you to consider the accuracy of a view, which is strong and direct. You should be familiar with the approach by now. In essence this involves presenting a case for the view and than a case against it, before reaching a balanced conclusion. The last two questions suggest a more evaluative approach from the outset although in reality you will still need to consider an argument for and an argument against the view.

Source-based questions on Chapter 6

I Napoleon and the Empire

Read carefully the five sources on pages 106–7, and answer the following questions:

a) Explain briefly in the context of each source the meaning of the following: *l'agglomération*, enlightened, common people. (*6 marks*)
b) In what way do the two sources relating to Holland provide differing insights into French rule? (*6 marks*)
c) What do the sources reveal about Napoleon's attitudes towards his conquered subjects? (*8 marks*)
d) 'Napoleonic rule in Europe helped promote nationalism.' Explain why you agree or disagree with this opinion. (*10 marks*)

In part **a** you will need to explain briefly and concisely the meaning of each word or phrase. Provide a clear and simple explanation that, if possible, contains some factual knowledge. When you are attempting to explain the differing insights in **b**, consider the first source and draw out from it the points which you wish to make, then consider the other source and do the same. This will provide a clear answer for the examiner. Remember to quote any relevant points and also, where it is relevant, consider who is writing to whom. The best approach to adopt for part **c** is to consider an overview – what relevant points can be drawn from the sources as a whole, rather than trawling your way through each one in sequence. Part **d** invites you to adopt one view and to argue in favour of it. Use material from the sources and, where relevant, additional background knowledge to support your answer.

7 Napoleon and Europe: Collapse c. 1810–15

POINTS TO CONSIDER

From the height of his power in Europe in early 1810, Napoleon and his empire collapsed in spectacular fashion. The central theme of this chapter is the mix of factors that contributed to this decline and fall. Focus carefully on two key issues: firstly the decisions taken by Napoleon that might have undermined his position, and secondly the strength and tenacity of the opposing powers. As you read through the chapter try to decide which of these factors was the most important. Note how the map of Europe changed following the collapse of the empire.

KEY DATES

1808	**August**	British expeditionary force under Wellington reaches Portugal
1810	**9 July**	Annexation of Holland
	31 December	Tsar Alexander breaks the Continental Blockade
1811		Wellington drives Masséna out of Portugal (winter/spring)
		Preparations begin for war with Russia (autumn)
1812	**24 June**	Invasion of Russia – *Grande Armée* crosses Niemen
	7 September	Battle of Borodino
	14 September	Napoleon enters Moscow
	19 October	Retreat from Moscow commences
	22–23 October	General Malet's conspiracy in Paris
	16 December	Remnant of *Grand Armée* re-crosses the Niemen
1813	**28 February**	Prussia signs alliance with Russia
	June	Wellington defeats French at Vittoroa; Joseph flees to France
	12 August	Austria joins Prussia and Russia
	16–19 October	Battle of Leipzig
	17 November	Uprising against Napoleon in Holland
1814	**30–31 March**	Fall of Paris
	6 April	Napoleon abdicates; Bourbons restored
	3 May	Exile of Napoleon to Elba
1815	**1 March**	Napoleon lands in France – start of 'Hundred Days'
	18 June	Battle of Waterloo
	22 June	Second Abdication
	17 October	Napoleon lands in St Helena

1 Towards Defeat 1808–12

> **KEY ISSUES** How significant was the war in Spain for Napoleon's defeat? What impact did the invasion of Russia have on Napoleon?

Although the frontiers of 1807 were not those of the Empire at its greatest extent, that year marked an important turning point in Napoleon's affairs. He was at the peak of success, with his three mainland enemies brought to heel and with the expectation that Britain would soon succumb to the Continental Blockade. In November 1807 Russia declared war on her former ally, Britain. An anti-French coalition was therefore unlikely in the short term. Napoleon was in the ascendant. There were still victories to come and conquests to be made, but only at an increased cost in men and materials; and, significantly, there were to be disasters and defeats. The general trend from 1808 onwards was no longer upward. Decline did not, however, set in immediately.

In one of his last successful military forays, at the beginning of 1808, Napoleon invaded and occupied the Papal States in an attempt to force the Pope to impose the Continental Blockade:

> His Holiness is sovereign of Rome, but I am the Emperor. My enemies must be his enemies. When Charlemagne made the popes temporal sovereigns he meant them to remain vassals of the [Holy Roman] Empire; nowadays far from regarding themselves as vassals of the Empire, they refuse to belong to it at all ... In the circumstances the only possible course was to occupy Rome with troops ... and to reduce the popes to their proper rank ...

The acquisition of the Papal States consolidated Napoleon's hold over Italy, all of which, apart from the island of Sicily, was now French. Although the Empire continued to grow until 1811, a decline in Napoleon's fortunes was evident from 1808 onwards. Among the causes were his two great 'mistakes' – the Spanish and Russian campaigns. Both, like the invasion of the Papal States, were brought about by his policy of enforcing the Continental Blockade along the whole European coast line, from the Mediterranean to the White Sea. While British sea-power remained superior, Napoleon had no chance of defeating Britain by direct military means. The best he could hope for was to use his land-based power as an economic weapon by making use of his control over the European coastline to prevent British trade with Europe.

a) The Peninsular War – 'the Spanish Ulcer'

The Peninsular war (fought in the Iberian peninsula, which included Portugal as well as Spain) resulted in the eventual loss of about half of the French soldiers who served there. It also failed totally in its primary objective, of enforcing the Continental Blockade. Despite over-

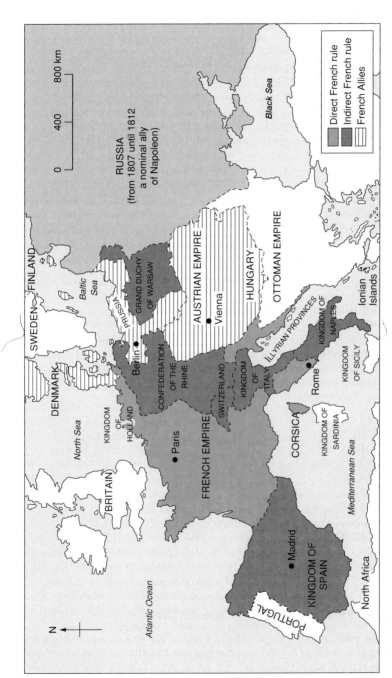

Europe 1810

running Portugal in 1807, the Blockade was not effective. The value of British exports entering Europe through Portuguese ports actually doubled between 1808 and 1809 to nearly a million pounds, and by 1811 the annual total had increased to more than 6 million.

Franco-Spanish relations between 1799 and 1807 were for the most part strained. Napoleon informed Spain that her position was simply that of a French ally whose duty was to supply men and money as and when required. Spain was a country with a large yet rather unstable empire that was ruled by a weak monarchy and a corrupt administration. The wealth of the country was largely in the hands of the church and the aristocracy. Napoleon believed that Spain could be bound more closely to France without too much difficulty. But as Felix Markham notes, 'Napoleon's initial and persistent error was in assuming that there was a substantial middle class in Spain which would welcome enlightened reform on the French model'.[1] This proved to be a very costly assumption. In 1808 Napoleon removed the Spanish king and his heir, and substituted a ruler of his own choice whom he could control, his brother Joseph. There were a number of consequences to this decision:

- Large numbers of ordinary Spanish people rose in revolt against French rule.
- Maintaining garrisons in Spain proved to be a significant drain on French military resources.
- The Franco-Spanish attack on Portugal prompted Britain to commit military forces to defend her ally.
- Napoleon's inability to resolve the situation cast doubts on his military and political judgement.

Joseph, previously the popular King of Naples, was gravely disappointed on arrival in Spain. 'Not a single Spaniard is on my side' he wrote, while Murat led an army to occupy Madrid and impose French rule. Murat handled a revolt by the people of Madrid in May 1808 with great ferocity and 100 Spaniards were executed in retaliation for the killing of 31 Frenchmen. The scene was immortalised by Goya's horrific painting, and helped rouse the whole population to patriotic anger against the French occupying forces (see page 121). Local resistance committees (*juntas*) were set up, co-ordinated by the clergy and members of the nobility, to raise guerilla fighters and regular soldiers. A small and comparatively inexperienced French army was defeated at Baylen by a force of Spanish regular troops. The sensation created by this defeat brought Napoleon himself to Spain with 100,000 veterans of the *Grande Armée*. A British expeditionary force was despatched to the Peninsula in answer to a Spanish request for help and quickly drove the French out of Portugal.

The nature of the war conducted in the Iberian Peninsula was brutal in the extreme. It was characterised by the emergence of what became well established in the twentieth century (particularly in relation to liberation struggles), namely *guerrilla* warfare. The Spanish

The Shootings of May Third 1808 by Francisco Goya

word *guerrilla* means a small war fought by irregular forces drawing supplies and support from the local population. In 1812 it was estimated that there were between 33,000 and 50,000 Spanish irregular forces engaged in the campaign against Napoleon. The arrival of Wellington in Portugal in 1808 had a profound impact on the nature of the struggle. Wellington's army numbered some 35,000 men and, because they lacked both artillery and cavalry, they relied heavily on *guerrilla* forces. He proved to be a formidable opponent, and although a cautious commander he was able to exploit French weaknesses regarding lack of supplies while at the same time fully exploiting British naval supremacy to re-supply and reinforce his own forces. In 1810–11 Marshal Massena attacked Lisbon, failed in his objective and suffered 25,000 casualties in the process. As Wellington shrewdly observed in 1811, there were 353,000 French troops in Spain and yet they had no authority beyond the spot where they stood.

Napoleon, distracted by news of Austrian mobilisation on the Danube, left Spain at the beginning of 1809. Without his leadership and with no other supreme commander, the war was left in the hands of mutually hostile generals. The aimable Joseph did his best to pacify his unwilling subjects, with a fair amount of success, but in 1810 much of this conciliatory work was undone by Napoleon, who did not trust such softness. Without consultation, he removed large areas of the country from Joseph's control and turned them into semi-independent military frontier provinces.

Wellington made little impact on the general European conflict. Britain was unable to prevent the defeat of Austria in 1809 or the invasion of Russia in 1812. In the wake of France's military commitment and disasters in Russia however, Wellington moved on the offensive. In 1812 he captured Ciudad Rodrigo and Badajoz. Following the defeat of Marmont at Salamanca he entered Madrid. Northern Spain was liberated in 1813 following his victory at Vittoria. French forces were driven back across the Pyrenees and finally defeated at Toulouse in 1814.

The war in Spain was never popular in France. France's defeat in the Iberian Peninsula was brought about by a combination of conventional and irregular methods of waging war.[2] While it eroded French military prestige, the long, drawn out campaign against *guerillas* was both expensive and demoralising. It is aptly called the 'Spanish Ulcer': a wound that weakens the victim without ever being fatal. In addition to weakening France, the Peninsular war relieved the pressure on Britain. The economic damage to the British economy from the Continental System was eased. Access to Spanish markets in Europe and South America helped boost British exports to £48 million in 1810 (from £38 million in 1808). As Paul Kennedy notes, 'the security of the British Isles and its *relative* prosperity on the one hand, and the overstretched and increasingly grasping nature of French rule on the other, at last interacted to bring down Napoleon's empire'.[3]

Had Napoleon remained in Spain in January 1809 it is possible that he could have gained victory in a rapid campaign. He himself said afterwards that he ought to have stayed another month, establishing his authority and taking the initiative. The delay in reaching the Danube that this would have caused would have meant sacrificing gains there, and it may be that by 1809 Napoleon had decided that Spain was not worth such sacrifices. If so, then his mistake was leaving the army locked in a worthless conflict – was he too proud to withdraw them, admit failure and leave Spain to govern herself? – when he could so easily have solved the problem of how to stop British goods entering Europe through the Peninsula. All he needed to do was close his Pyrenees border with Spain. Difficult mountain country it might be to patrol effectively, but surely, with much of it impassable, it was easier to do this than guard 3000 miles of open coastline. He need never have invaded Spain at all to achieve his declared objective; but perhaps the temptation of adding yet another satellite to his list was irresistible.

b) The Defeat of Austria

Elsewhere during 1809–11 the French army was doing rather better. After leaving Spain, Napoleon reached the Danube valley in early March 1809, where he waited for the Austrians, whose army had been much strengthened since the defeats of 1805–6 and was now led by the extremely able Archduke Charles. (Wellington thought the Archduke the best general of the age and said of him: 'He knows more about it than all of us put together'.) The campaign lasted just under two months. In April the Austrians were defeated at Eckmühl with severe losses, while in May Napoleon, after successfully occupying Vienna, was equally heavily defeated at Aspern (Essling) and had to retire to a nearby island in the Danube. With honours even, a third encounter took place in mid-July at Wagram. It was the last of Napoleon's great victories. A pitched battle ended in an Austrian retreat and a request for an armistice. In October the Treaty of Schönbrunn was signed. It was a dictated peace in typical Napoleonic style. By it Austria lost the Illyrian provinces on the Adriatic coast, with their population of 3.5 million, her army was reduced to 150,000 and she was forced to find an indemnity of nearly £4 million. When the Austrian Emperor complained about the severity of the terms, Napoleon merely replied that if Austria had kept the peace made in 1801 at Lunéville, 'both countries might have been spared many sufferings'.

At the end of 1809 Napoleon decided to divorce Josephine and remarry in the hope of fathering an heir for the Empire. Proposals for marriage with the Tsar's sister fell through, and the Austrian Emperor,who 'will shrink from nothing that may contribute to the welfare and peace of the state', offered his daughter, Marie-Louise, as a replacement. In March 1810, before the bride left for France, a proxy marriage took place in Vienna at which the bridegroom was represented by Napoleon's recent enemy, Archduke Charles! Austria and France might have officially become allies but the new Empress received only a lukewarm welcome in Paris. It was reported that the crowd that saw her arrive 'had been attracted only out of simple curiosity and showed neither enthusiasm nor joy'. She was, after all, the niece of Marie-Antoinette.

c) The Invasion of Russia 1812

The Franco-Russian *rapprochement* made at Tilsit in 1807 was not easy to maintain and both sides felt uncomfortable about the relationship. There were a number of issues that caused friction between the two countries and led to a resumption of hostilities. The main factors that led to conflict were:

- Mutual distrust of each other's hostile expansionist aims in the Baltic, central Europe and the Balkans.
- Napoleon's refusal to support the Tsar's ambitions to seize Istanbul – he had similar aspirations of his own.
- The Austrian marriage annoyed the Tsar, as did Napoleon's annexation of the North German coast and the Duchy of Oldenburg (the Tsar's sister was married to the Crown Duke) especially as the Duchy's independence had been guaranteed at Tilsit.
- Alexander attacked Sweden with French encouragement, but without French agreement seized and annexed Swedish Finland.
- There were arguments over the future of the Grand Duchy of Warsaw.
- The main disagreement arose over the Tsar's virtual withdrawal from the Continental Blockade. On the last day of 1810 he introduced a new trade tariff that discriminated against France and in favour of Britain.

Napoleon determined on war to restore his dominance over the Tsar and to reinforce the Continental Blockade. The army Napoleon gathered to invade Russia was the largest he ever assembled. It was also one of the most cosmopolitan forces created since the time of the crusades in the twelfth century. The *Grande Armée* of 600,000 consisted of Germans, Swiss, Spanish, Portuguese, Italians, Poles and Lithuanians. Only about 270,000 of the total were Frenchmen. Michael Broers argues that whereas Napoleon had clear political reasons for invading Russia, he had never before gone to war with such ill-defined military goals. 'In truth, the defined objectives of the campaign of 1812 did not extend much beyond catching a Russian army and defeating it in the field'.[4] Napoleon had never before commanded such a large force, over such a vast area. During the course of the campaign he was inexplicably indecisive and lethargic at critical moments.[5]

In June 1812, without any declaration of war, Napoleon crossed the River Niemen. He was unable to use his usual strategy of luring the enemy towards him, and forcing a decisive battle early in the campaign. The much smaller Russian armies continually retreated before him destroying food supplies as they went. Napoleon was therefore drawn ever deeper into Russia, extending his supply lines and increasing the difficulties for his large, slow-moving force of catching up with the enemy. Medical supplies and food were short, and disease struck down 60,000 men even before the campaign had properly begun. The Russian army's scorched-earth tactic meant that Napoleon found it difficult to feed his men – they were unable to live off the country – and over 1000 cavalry horses died from eating unripe corn in the fields.

By the time Napoleon reached Vitebsk his army was demoralised. It had already suffered the same number of casualties, either from disease or being picked off by skirmishing Cossacks, as would be expected from large battles. By mid-August the central army group commanded by Napoleon had lost nearly 100,000 men. Pressing on to Smolensk they found the city had already been destroyed by the Russians and that no food or shelter was available there. The recently appointed Russian commander, the one-eyed Kutusov, urged on by the Tsar, now decided to stand and fight, and waited with an army of about 120,000 west of Moscow near the village of Borodino. There on 7 September, in a day-long battle of enormous ferocity, Napoleon won a technical victory after a prolonged artillery duel, but at great cost in men and guns. The French lost 30,000 men, and Kutusov's army 50,000. In his Order of the Day Napoleon, parodying Henry V at Agincourt, declared: 'Let them say this of you: He was present at this great battle under the walls of Moscow' (only the walls were still sixty miles away!). On 14 September Napoleon's advance guard rode into a largely deserted Moscow. The rest of the army followed, 'all clapping their hands and shouting, Moscow, Moscow'. Two days later, two-thirds of the city was in ruins, burnt down by fires started on orders of the Russian governor in order to destroy food and ammunition supplies. The Tsar refused to negotiate despite the loss of Moscow. Another Tilsit was impossible to contemplate in the patriotic fervour of the moment.

The unusually mild autumn tempted Napoleon to linger in Moscow for over a month. He ignored the warnings of bad weather to come, and only the eventual realisation that the *Grande Armée* would starve to death if he stayed longer in the ruined and empty city caused him to order a return home. Laden with loot and slowed down by their wounded, the army began the retreat on 19 October. Napoleon ordered them to take a route to the south of the one by which they had arrived, in the hope that there he would find in an unravaged countryside food and shelter for his men who now numbered only 107,000; but attacks by the waiting Russian army soon pushed the French north again and back onto their original route. This forced them to march over the battlefield of Borodino, still strewn with the stripped and decaying bodies of 30,000 of their own dead.

The Retreat from Moscow, 1812

Nothing in the world more saddening, more distressing. One saw heaped bodies of men, women and children: soldiers of all arms, all nations, choked by the fugitives or hit by Russian grapeshot; horses, carriages, guns, ammunition wagons, abandoned carts. One cannot imagine a more terrifying sight than the appearance of the two broken bridges, and the river frozen right to the bottom. Immense riches lay scattered on this shore of death.

Peasants and Cossacks prowled around these piles of dead, removing whatever was most valuable ... Both sides of the road were piled with the dead in all positions, or with men dying of cold, hunger, exhaustion, their uniforms in tatters, and beseeching us to take them prisoner. However much we might have wished to help, unfortunately we could do nothing.

From the memoirs of a French emigré, General Comte de Rochechouart, who was serving with the Russian Imperial Guard, 1812

By the time Napoleon reached Smolensk in mid-November there were only 50,000 left in the *Grande Armée* itself. Sickness and skirmishers, famine and exhaustion had taken their toll, and the winter had only just begun to bite. In snow and intense cold the army, now further depleted, left Smolensk and marched west. The Russians reached the River Beresina (a tributary of the Niemen) before the French, and demolished the bridges. Thus prevented from escaping, Napoleon's army faced destruction. That anything of the *Grande Armée* and its auxiliary troops survived was due to Napoleon's discovery of a ford and the building of two emergency trestle bridges across the river in appalling conditions. In the panic to reach safety, after the bridges were destroyed to prevent a Russian pursuit, many were drowned in the freezing water. Thousands more, together with the main mass of camp followers and their goods, were left behind on the bank to the mercy of the Russians. Of the 40,000 men of the *Grande Armée* who got safely across the bridges some 25,000 survived to reach Germany at the end of the year.

c) Assessment

Despite the version of events put out by Napoleon in his famous 29th Bulletin, that it was the snow and ice, the intense cold and the frostbite that destroyed the *Grande Armée*, this was not so. The army, together with its auxiliaries, was destroyed long before winter arrived in the first days of November. Twice as many men (35,000) were lost on the retreat in a week of fair weather in late October as were lost in a week of snow and ice on the road from Smolensk to the Beresina in mid-November. Even more instructive is the fact that 350,000 (more than half the total French forces) died *before* they reached Moscow.

Napoleon lost his army by bad management, poor supply arrangements, lack of local knowledge, and over-confidence. He had allowed himself nine weeks to defeat Russia and return in triumph to Germany. His army had only summer clothing and enough food for three weeks (he intended to be comfortably ensconced in Moscow as Emperor of the East by then). Many supplies proved inadequate or non-existent. There was no fodder for the horses, nor frost nails for their shoes, no maps covering more than a few miles inside the Russian border, and no bandages for the wounded. There was unusual confusion in the French army command, too. General Caulincourt wrote after leaving Moscow, 'Never was a retreat worse planned, or carried out with less discipline; never did convoys march so badly … To lack of forethought we owed a great part of our disaster'. The fragility of the imperial government was exposed by the Malet affair (22–23 October 1812) when a plot by a former general almost succeeded in persuading some key officials that the Emperor was dead and a provisional government needed to be formed. But the ruse failed to convince everyone and the plotters were arrested and quickly executed.[6]

2 The Last Campaigns 1813–15

> **KEY ISSUE** What were the reasons for the final defeat of Napoleon?

a) The Allies United: The Fourth Coalition 1813–15

The Russian disaster encouraged a general diplomatic realignment, which began in February 1813 with the signing of an anti-French alliance by Russia and Prussia. Tsar Alexander now saw himself as the saviour of Europe. Under his leadership a Fourth Coalition, was formed consisting initially of Russia, Prussia and Britain. It was still not a full alliance, being based only on separate bilateral treaties between Britain and Russia and Britain and Prussia. In the early summer of 1813 a Russo-Prussian campaign in central Europe met with some success and in June Napoleon – with a much weakened army after his losses in Russia, and forced to fight on two fronts by the continued conflict in Spain – accepted Austrian proposals for an armistice and a peace conference. Austria's attitude towards the Fourth Coalition had so far been one of hesitant suspicion. The Chancellor, Metternich, distrusted Russo-Prussian ambitions in Germany, and Napoleon's marriage to Marie-Louise had left Austria in an awkward position as a nominal ally of France; but in August 1813 Austria, tired of Napoleon's unwillingness to negotiate a peace settlement, declared war on France. It was the first occasion on which *all* the other great powers, Britain, Russia, Prussia and Austria, were at war with Napoleon at the same time, though there was still no single alliance binding them together.

Final negotiations in Prague for a possible general peace treaty came to nothing – Napoleon would make no concessions, would surrender no territory. He could perhaps even at this late date have obtained peace on reasonable terms, retaining at least France's 'natural frontiers', and he might himself have continued as ruler of France. However, he seems to have feared that a negotiated settlement would mean the end of his power, for he was not one of the hereditary sovereigns of Europe. They, he said, could lose 20 battles and keep their thrones; he, as an upstart soldier, could not. 'My domination will not survive the day when I cease to be strong and therefore feared'. War, rather than diplomacy, had always been his preference, and characteristically he chose to stake his all on military victory to settle the issue of his future.

The end of the armistice led to renewed fighting, and in October the numerical superiority of the combined armies of Austria, Prussia and Russia enabled them to win a decisive but expensive victory at Leipzig in the three-day 'Battle of the Nations'. Outnumbered, Napoleon was heavily defeated and forced back to the Rhine. His influence in Germany gone, the Grand Empire was starting to unravel. One after another, Baden, Bavaria, Würtemberg and the other states of the Confederation went over to the Allies; Jerôme was driven out of Westphalia; Saxony fell into Prussian hands and the Grand Duchy of Warsaw into those of Russia. As the news of the battle spread so did the disintegration of the Empire. Within the week a popular revolt in Amsterdam drove the French out of Holland; the Illyrian Provinces had to be abandoned soon after; Spain was already lost, the last of Napoleon's forces there streaming back into France and final defeat. Only Belgium, Switzerland and Italy now constituted the Empire.

One of his generals met Napoleon shortly after the battle:

He was sunk in gloom – with reason. Hardly two months had elapsed and an immense army of 400,000 men had melted away in his hands – for the second time in a year the world was presented with a spectacle of destruction … only about 60,000 men remained. [On reaching the Rhine an outbreak of typhus killed about a third of these survivors.]

Napoleon's only hope was that Austria, Prussia and Russia would quarrel over the future of Germany and Poland and that the coalition would collapse as a result. This was Britain's fear, but it was averted when intense diplomatic pressure by the British government led to the imposition of the Treaty of Chaumont on the coalition in March 1814. This treaty, which converted the coalition into a Quadruple Alliance, committed each of the four powers not to conclude a separate peace but to fight on until Napoleon was defeated. They would then remain in alliance for 20 years while political and territorial plans, outlined in the treaty, were put into effect in a post-Napoleonic Europe. At long last the allies had come together in a properly united alliance of powers legally bound to each other in a common purpose.

In France there was discontent and opposition as preparations began in bitter winter weather for a new campaign. Napoleon set to work to raise yet another army and to find the money to equip it. The financial situation was desperate, and the burden of conscription had become intolerable in a country that had been at war for 20 years. Despite the fact that for the first time since 1792 France was facing invasion by the 'kings' of old Europe, reports made by the commissioners sent round the provinces by Napoleon showed that public morale was very low. The people wanted peace; Napoleon wanted victory. He suspected the Allies' motives in renewing the offer of a settlement on the basis of the 'natural frontiers', and demanded more. His envoy despaired:

> The Emperor did not see, or rather would not see, his true position. He deceived himself ... about his own strength. He could not forget that he had once dictated to Europe, or reconcile himself to the idea of being dictated to in his own turn.

By the middle of January 1814, when Napoleon finally agreed to negotiate, it was too late. The Allied offer had been withdrawn. There followed a campaign to defend the Rhine frontier during which Napoleon won a number of small but impressive victories. These successes, though, were not enough to stop the enemy advance, and at the end of March the allies entered Paris along with the newly restored Bourbon King Louis XVIII. Napoleon's obstinacy had lost him everything. He agreed, unwillingly, to abdicate:

> The allied powers having proclaimed the Emperor Napoleon to be the sole obstacle to the re-establishment of peace in Europe, the Emperor Napoleon, faithful to his word, declares that he renounces for himself and his heirs the thrones of France and Italy, and that there is no personal sacrifice, even life itself, which he is not ready to make for the good of France.

An attempt at suicide having failed – the poison, which he had carried round with him for emergency use on the Russian campaign, had been kept too long and had lost its potency – Napoleon took it as a sign for the future. 'Fate has decided that I must live and await all that Providence has in store for me. I abdicate and I yield nothing.' The terms of Napoleon's future were settled by the Treaty of Fontainbleau. Napoleon, largely through the mediation of Tsar Alexander I was granted the sovereignty of the Island of Elba and a pension.[7]

b) Final Defeat and End of Napoleonic Europe

Following his abdication the future of France and her Empire was discussed at Vienna. The first Treaty of Paris (May 1814) began the long process of reaching a peace settlement by reducing France to her 1792 borders. Almost immediately after the treaty was signed the allies fell out with one another. Matters became so acrimonious that Britain and Austria, encouraged by the restored Bourbon government of France, made a secret alliance against Prussia and Russia. Ten months later Napoleon was back, sensing an opportunity to split the allies and recover his throne. He proclaimed: 'The eagle will fly from steeple to steeple until it reaches the towers of Notre Dame'.

Austria and Britain, however, rejected his offers of separate negotiations, declared him an outlaw and aligned themselves with Prussia and Russia against him. An army of 125.000 men was raised. He needed a quick military victory to unite France behind him and to reassert his authority over the country. His immediate targets were the two allied armies in Belgium under Wellington and the Prussian General, Blucher. His aim was to defeat them before they could combine with significant numbers of Austrian and Russian forces heading towards France. Napoleon issued what was to be his last Order of the Day on 14 June 1815: 'Soldiers ... the Allies have begun the most unjust of aggressions. let us march to meet them ... for every Frenchman with a heart, the moment has come to conquer or perish'.

On 18 June one of the decisive battles in European history was fought near the Belgian village of Waterloo. Napoleon had a slight numerical advantage over Wellington, 72,000 men to 68,000. The outcome of this evenly balanced struggle was ultimately determined in favour of the allies by the arrival of the Prussians. As Wellington said the next day 'it was a damned close thing – the nearest run thing you ever saw in your life'

Undaunted, Napoleon at once began planning a new campaign: 'all is not lost. I suppose that when I reassemble my forces I shall have ... 150,000 men ready immediately to bring against the enemy. I will use carriage horses to drag the guns, raise another 100,000 men by conscription, arm them with muskets taken from the royalists ...'. It was not to be. 'We are not going to begin all over again' was the comment by the Council of State. Without political or popular support Napoleon had no option but to agree to demands for his second abdication. His proposal that a Regency should be set up for Napoleon II, his young son, was ignored. On 8 July Louis XVIII made his second entry into Paris. After Napoleon's final abdication and exile in June, the second Treaty of Paris (November 1815) reduced the frontiers of France still further, to those of 1790. The First Empire was finally at an end.

There remained the problem of the territories of the French Empire and of the satellite states. Each of the allies had different views on what should be done and great power unity was constantly threatened by suspicion and disagreement. However, it was accepted by all the allies that France needed to be contained within her revised frontiers and that this could be best done by surrounding her with a ring of buffer states – not the weak and feeble neighbours who had collapsed in 1792–3, but strong, potentially hostile states who would prevent any future French aggression. To the south, Austrian influence was restored in northern Italy (in Lombardy and Venice), and a newly strengthened kingdom of Sardinia-Piedmont (including Nice, Genoa and Savoy) guarded the Italian frontier with France; to the north, Belgium was united with an independent Holland behind a fortified frontier with France; while to the east, Switzerland's guaranteed independence barred the way, as did the Rhinelands, now a part of Prussia. In this way the frontiers that France had threatened most often during the seventeenth and eighteenth centuries were blocked off.

As far as the satellite states were concerned it was a generally, though not completely, conservative settlement. In Italy Naples was returned to Bourbon rule and the other states were restored to their pre-1796 boundaries and mostly to their former ruling families. The Papal States were returned to the Pope. In Germany Napoleon's suppression of a large number of minor German states was confirmed and 41 (later reduced to 38) sovereign states were brought together in a new German Confederation, whose borders were not dissimilar to those of the old Holy Roman Empire. Russia acquired most of Poland and Spain was returned to Bourbon rule. The map of Europe again looked much the same as it had done in the eighteenth century. Geographically, Napoleonic Europe had disappeared.

3 Military Factors in Napoleon's Decline and Fall 1808–15

> **KEY ISSUE** How did military and strategic factors help bring about Napoleon's downfall?

There were changes in the military organisation and methods of warfare of both Napoleon and his enemies after 1807. In that year the *Grande Armée* was still strong enough to defeat all who stood in its way, Austrians, Prussians or Russians. It had, however, lost many of its experienced and disciplined troops and, although new recruits were available to fill the gaps, they went into battle untrained and often unreliable. The French army had been created as a national army, but by 1807 its character had changed. It had become increasingly cosmopolitan. Two-thirds of the men were either non-French troops from the annexed territories or foreign auxiliaries from the satellite states of the Grand Empire. As a result, Napoleon's earlier tactics of attack by mixed columns of infantry and skirmishers were no longer so successful. This was because high casualty levels resulted in poor quality replacement conscripts. After 1807 Napoleon like his predecessors resorted to crude attack columns thrown at enemy lines with little concern for casualty rates. His tactical options were increasingly limited and he began to rely much more on sustained artillery barrages. As his armies became larger – over 600,000 crossed the Niemen

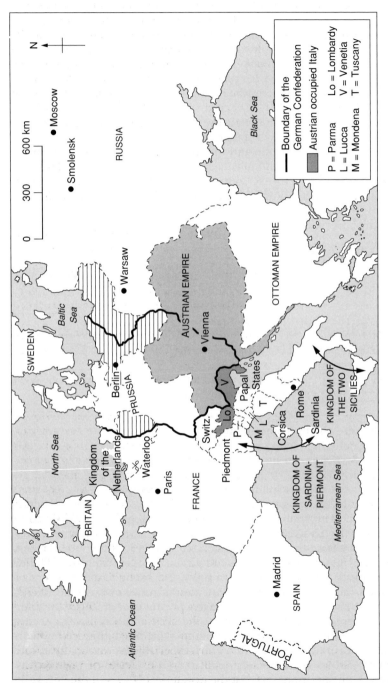

Europe 1815

into Russia with him in 1812 – they were more difficult to manoeuvre and to provision on the march. His later campaigns had, therefore, to depend much less on the surprise elements of speed and mobility than before, and his battles to rely much more on the sheer brute force of artillery duels or the weight of numbers storming the enemy lines in a massed charge of cavalry or infantry. His later victories were much costlier in men than the earlier ones. For example, 30,000 were lost at Wagram in 1809 compared with the 8000 lost at Austerlitz in 1805. French losses overall in the Austrian campaign of 1809 were almost equal to those of the enemy.

While the rest of Europe continued to employ old-fashioned methods Napoleon's new-style armies had been invincible. This situation did not last. His enemies learnt to play Napoleon at his own game. They made a number of important changes, to enable them to defeat Napoleon:

- Copying Napoleon's tactics, his enemies became more flexible in their approach and developed their artillery to match his.
- They increased the size of their armies to equal or exceed his.
- Prussia and Austria, after their disastrous defeats, replaced their old foreign mercenary armies with new national ones, designed to have a new structure, armaments and equipment in accordance with the new methods of warfare.
- New methods were adopted to pin Napoleon down to a more defensive style of warfare, by denying him the opportunity to force an early and potentially decisive battle.
- Co-operation among the allies enabled them to field a combined force of superior manpower to Napoleon.

To some extent Napoleon played into their hands by the 'mistakes' of the Spanish and Russian ventures, brought about by his determination to force both countries to implement the Continental Blockade against Britain. In both cases he grossly underestimated the sheer size of the country he was hoping to conquer, and was ill-informed about both the terrain and the climate he would encounter. Accustomed to allowing his armies to 'live off the land' in countries they were campaigning in, he wrongly expected they could do so in Spain and Russia. In Spain *guerrilla* fighters, and in Russia scorched earth policies, produced unexpected difficulties for the French troops. The 'Spanish ulcer' eventually cost Napoleon about 300,000 men and 3000 million francs in gold, and brought the first serious defeats for his armies. In Russia matters were even worse: nearly 500,000 men dead, missing or taken prisoner, and 200,000 trained horses and 1000 guns lost – all in the course of a campaign lasting only six months. This enormous expenditure of experienced officers and men weakened the French army, especially the cavalry, for future campaigns, leaving it over-dependent on new levies of raw recruits. Even more important was that the disasters of 1812 and the defeats in the Peninsular War shattered Napoleon's reputation for military invincibility.

It had always been a weakness in his command structure that he did not take his senior officers into his confidence when on campaign, nor allow them any independence of action. He retained all power and all decision-making in his own hands. It was an entirely personal leadership. In the early campaigns, when his army was still quite small, this did not matter a great deal; but as armies became larger – already in 1806 Napoleon was at the head of an army at Jena of about 165,000 men – personal control over the entire field of operations became more difficult to achieve. Even then Napoleon did not establish a permanent staff to share the command. He continued to tell his marshals what to do, and they continued to do it. As one of them remarked, 'the Emperor needs neither advice nor plans of campaign ... our duty is just to obey'. As a result when, as in Spain for instance, they were unavoidably left in charge in Napoleon's absence from the country, his senior staff proved quite unable to cope.

Caulincourt, one of Napoleon's trusted generals, who travelled everywhere with him on campaign, riding alongside his carriage as a privileged member of his entourage, and who knew as much as anybody was ever permitted to know about the Emperor, wrote illuminatingly of his strengths and weaknesses in the field:

> On campaign he was awakened for everything. Even the Chief of Staff who received and dispatched and knew the Emperor's plans, decided nothing ... The Emperor occupied himself with the most minute details. He wanted everything to bear the imprint of his genius ... no detail seemed too humble to escape his attention ... The distinctive numbers of his regiments, his army service companies, his baggage battalions were all classified in his brain most marvellously. He knew where each one was, when it started and when it should arrive at its destination. Never did a man combine such a memory with a more creative genius. But his creative genius had no knowledge of conserving its forces ... If a thirty-days' campaign did not produce the results of a year's fighting, the greater part of his calculations were upset by the losses he suffered, for everything was done so rapidly and unexpectedly, the chiefs under him had so little experience, showed so little care and were, in addition, so spoiled by former successes, that everything was disorganized, wasted and thrown away ... This habit of victory cost us dear when we got to Russia and even dearer when we were in retreat; the glorious habit of marching ever forward made us veritable schoolboys when it came to retreating.

In a similar vein, Metternich, the Austrian Chancellor, wrote of what he saw as the major reason for Napoleon's initial success and eventual failure:

Napoleon did not fail to reckon largely on the weakness and errors of his adversaries. It must be confessed that a long experience only too well justified him in following this principle. But it is also certain that he abused it, and that the habit of despising the means and capabilities of his adversaries was one of the principal causes of his downfall. The Alliance of 1813 destroyed him, because he was never able to persuade himself that the members of a coalition could remain united and persevere in a given course of action.

By 1814 Napoleon's early self-confidence and determination had degenerated into supreme egoism, obstinacy and an unwillingness to face facts – a fatal combination for a commander about to meet for the first time a united enemy able to deploy a numerically superior combined force. The wars had become a case of France against the rest, with the result that Napoleon was faced with odds that even he could not prevail against. As Charles Esdaile concludes, the major European powers decided to fight fire with fire by reforming their armies. 'France was confronted with new "nations-in-arms" at a time when, thanks to Napoleon, she had ceased to be one herself.'[8]

References

1 Felix Markham, *Napoleon* (Mentor, 1963) p. 172.
2 Charles Esdaile, 'The British Army and the Guerrilla War in Spain' in *The Road to Waterloo* (Alan Sutton, 1990) p. 133.
3 Paul Kennedy, *The Rise and Fall of the Great Powers* (Fontana, 1988) p. 175.
4 Michael Broers, *Europe Under Napoleon 1799–1815* (Arnold, 1996) p. 235.
5 D.M.G. Sutherland, *The French Revolution and Empire* (Blackwell, 2003) p. 367.
6 See Jean Tulard, *Napoleon: The Myth of the Saviour* (Methuen, 1984) p. 316 for further details.
7 Vincent Cronin, *Napoleon* (Penguin, 1971) p. 457.
8 Charles J. Esdaile *The French Wars 1792–1816* (Routledge, 2001) p. 85.

Summary Diagram
Why was Napoleon Defeated?

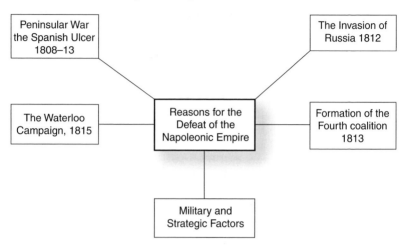

Peninsular War
the Spanish Ulcer
1808–13

The Invasion of
Russia 1812

The Waterloo
Campaign, 1815

Reasons for the
Defeat of the
Napoleonic Empire

Formation of the
Fourth coalition
1813

Military and
Strategic Factors

Working on Chapter 7

After having read this chapter, you will have completed your study of the history of the Napoleonic era in Europe. This is an important chapter as it seeks to provide you with the various reasons why Napoleon was defeated and his empire brought down. For revision purposes you may find it useful to identify the main points on a sheet of paper with perhaps one or two sentences under each to note the most important facts. For discussion purposes you could arrange these in rank order and justify the position of each.

Answering structured and essay questions on Chapter 7

Essay and structured questions on this chapter will mainly focus on seeking to explain why Napoleon was defeated. Before attempting these, ensure that you are fully aware of the various reasons and that you have a good working knowledge of the factual detail necessary to provide high level answers. Consider the following examples:

1 **a)** Explain two reasons why Napoleon was defeated. *(20 marks)*
   b) Why did opposition to Napoleonic rule grow during the period 1803–14? *(40 marks)*
2 **a)** Explain the impact of the Continental System on Europe. *(20 marks)*
   b) Compare the importance of the rise of nationalism and of the failure to defeat Britain in explaining Napoleon's defeat. *(40 marks)*

The following are some typical examples of essay questions on the content of this chapter:

1. To what extent was Napoleon successful in imposing his will over the rest of Europe?
2. 'There were few benefits from Napoleonic rule.' Discuss.
3. 'How far was the "Spanish Ulcer" responsible for the defeat of Napoleon?
4. 'The most significant factor in explaining the defeat of Napoleon was the Russian campaign of 1812.' Is this a valid explanation for the defeat of Napoleon?
5. To what extent was the Continental system responsible for the downfall of Napoleon?

Source-based questions on Chapter 7

1. Napoleon's tactics observed

Study the source on page 134 by Napoleon's general Caulincourt, and answer the questions that follow:

a) Explain the meaning of the following – '... the glorious habit of marching ever forward made us veritable schoolboys when it came to retreating'. (line 17) (*5 marks*)
b) What insights does Caulincourt provide about Napoleon's leadership? (*10 marks*)
c) What does this source, and others in the chapter, reveal about why the Napoleonic empire was ultimately defeated? (*15 marks*)

8 The Napoleonic Legend

POINTS TO CONSIDER

Napoleon continues to fascinate professional historians, students of history and interested members of the public in a way that shows no sign of diminishing. Now that you are familiar with the main features of Napoleon's extraordinary career – his rise and fall and his impact on France and Europe – the focus of this chapter is on the Napoleonic legend. Napoleon was very concerned about his place in history, and clearly history is very interested in him. From early on in his career he practised 'perception management', carefully cultivating, controlling and projecting his image through propaganda and the media. As you read this chapter, consider the various methods he adopted to achieve this, and how subsequently it gave rise to the Napoleonic legend. As you are nearing the end of your study of Napoleon, you should be able to form some view as to his legacy.

KEY DATES

1815	17 October	Napoleon lands on St Helena
1821	5 May	Death of Napoleon
1823		Las Casas publishes *Memorial de Sainte-Hélène*
1840	December	Napoleon's remains returned to France and re-interred in the Invalides in Paris
1848	December	Louis-Napoleon elected President of the Second Republic
1852	December	Second Empire established under Napoleon III
1927		Abel Gance epic film *Napoleon* released
1936		Georges Lefebvre publishes *Napoléon*
1944		Pieter Geyl publishes *Napoleon: For and Against*

From early on in his career Napoleon went to great lengths to project a favourable image of himself. This practice continued and was refined when he attained power. He was possibly the first ruler to use propaganda in a systematic way as a weapon of war.[1] Following his final defeat and imprisonment on the island of St Helena in 1815, he set out to explain and justify his actions in a series of lengthy dictated recollections. When these were published, they formed the basis of the 'Napoleonic legend' of which he himself had been the chief architect, and on which others were to build after his death.

1 Image and Reality

> **KEY ISSUES** What did Napoleon consider to be the benefits of
> propaganda? How did he seek to present his image?

The benefits of propaganda, as far as Napoleon was concerned, were
considerable:

- Projecting a favourable image of himself and the imperial dynasty
- Presenting France and its revolutionary achievements in a positive
  way to the citizens of other European states
- Spreading negative and hostile views of his enemies.

Napoleon used a number of methods to cultivate his image and to
spread his propaganda.[2] Firstly, the media was tightly controlled under
the Empire, with press censorship (see page 41) ensuring that only
favourable material was published. Napoleon took a direct role in issuing bulletins that were delivered to all prefects for display in their
departments, providing carefully crafted updates of the latest military
situation. Secondly, in the visual arts Napoleon employed painters to
depict his image in a range of positive ways. These variously projected
the Emperor as heroic, brave, powerful, magisterial and compassionate. Both these methods went some way towards creating a personality
cult and helped sow the seeds of the Napoleonic legend.

The beginnings of the legend can be traced back, before the successful *coup* of Brumaire, to the string of dazzling victories won by the
young Napoleon in Italy in 1796–7 – at Castiglioni, Arcola, Lodi,
Rivoli and Mantua – and to the use that he made of them and of the
Peace of Campo Formio. Although Napoleon played a central role in
these events, they were certainly embellished and exaggerated at the
time and later by a range of writers and artists.

As well as making proclamations and issuing orders of the day, he
published newsheets, full of disinformation, intended to boost army
morale, and to dishearten the enemy. These newsheets were widely
circulated, and their contents included exaggerated reports or bulletins on the favourable progress of the war, written by Napoleon himself. He also sent senior officers to Paris in relays to report personally
to the Directory on his victories, making sure that their tales lost
nothing in the telling and that the news was passed on to the Paris
press. When he returned to France in 1797 he was greeted as a hero.
The *Institut de France*, the leading scientific association in Europe,
honoured Napoleon by admitting him to their mathematics division,
and everywhere he went he was fêted. At a splendid ceremony in the
Luxembourg Palace he personally handed over the Treaty of Campo
Formio to the Directors.

This practice of issuing bulletins that were economical with the
truth continued throughout Napoleon's career. The Battle of Eylau is

a good example. It was the first battle in which some of his troops had run away, and his losses among the remainder of the army had been high, yet he managed by skilful manipulation of the facts to make it appear not a drawn encounter but a French victory. He denied Russian versions of the engagement, dictating 'an eye-witness account, translated from the German' as the one he wished to go down into history, sending home specially commissioned pictures of the action, and issuing bulletins in which he initially falsified the number of French dead, substituting 2000 for the real figure of 20,000. He finished by publishing the almost certainly fictitious 'last words of a French officer killed in the battle'. (They bear a close resemblance to other 'last words' used in earlier bulletins.) 'I die content, since victory is ours ... Tell the Emperor I have only one regret – that in a few moments I shall be beyond doing anything more in his service or for the glory of France'. There could be no place in the legend for a drawn battle, any more than for a defeat.

An important function of Napoleon's bulletins was to arouse national enthusiasm and encourage hatred of the enemy. Writing after Austerlitz, Napoleon described the 'horrible spectacle' of the retreat under artillery fire of 20,000 Russians, who, driven back, were drowned in an 'immense lake' amidst heartrending screams 'which still ring in our ears'. The account owes more to fiction than reality as the lake (which, far from immense, was quite small) was drained soon after the battle and only a few cannons, 150 dead horses and three bodies were found. The whole account was intended to throw disgrace on the British, 'those perfidious islanders who are responsible', and ended with: 'May the cowardly oligarchs in London be visited with punishment for so much suffering!' After the retreat from Moscow it was of course the Russian winter that, unjustly, was given the entire blame for the destruction of the *Grande Armée*. There always had to be a scapegoat to hand. In his very last bulletin, issued after Waterloo, Napoleon complained that Wellington, 'who ought not to have won', owed his victory only to 'a sudden and unexplained panic terror which swept the entire field, so that in a moment the [French] army had become nothing but a confused mass'.

The most blatant example of Napoleon tampering with the truth in a bulletin, however, was after the battle of Marengo in June 1800. This 'official' account is full of inconsistencies that turn a near-run defeat into an easy victory. Much worse, though, it quite cynically took away from the two army commanders, who broke the enemy line and won the battle, the credit due to them for the victory, and appropriated it to Napoleon himself. One interpretation is that he was perhaps uncertain of his position as *First Consul*. But more likely, he was simply concerned with his own advancement.

As well as manipulating public opinion in his favour, he sought to control men's minds in other ways: through education ('above all we must secure unity – we must be able to cast a whole generation in the same mould'); through the Imperial catechism (see page 61) with its cult of the Emperor ('he defends the state by the strength of his arm; he has become the Lord's Anointed'), and through propaganda of all kinds. He also exercised a negative influence by the use of censorship and the suppression of freedom of expression. The bulletins and articles published in the government newspaper, *Le Moniteur*, not only propounded the official and accepted view of events, but by 1806 had become the only news source on political or military matters available to the French people. No discussion of perceptions other than Napoleon's was possible since there were no other views available to discuss.

Misrepresentation was not the sole prerogative of the literary form. Official painters were recruited to portray Napoleon and his régime in the most flattering light. To this end he was aided by some of the greatest artists of the age. Two in particular stand out. Gros met Napoleon in 1796 during his Italian campaign and was responsible for producing a number of carefully honed images of the Emperor. In 1804 he completed *Bonaparte Visiting the Victims of the Plague at Jaffa*. The painting depicts an incident from the Egyptian campaign when Napoleon, at his most compassionate, visited and comforted sick soldiers at a hospital. The heroic Emperor is the theme of another work by Gros. *Napoleon at the Battle of Eylau* was clearly intended as a work of propaganda. It is a romanticised depiction of the indecisive battle, fought in a snowstorm in February 1807. Gros's version of the battlefield does not evoke the horrific reality of the 40,000 French and Russian dead, showing instead Napoleon the inspirer, motivator and comforter, among his beloved troops.

The greatest of Napoleon's image-makers was Jacques-Louis David. He often used considerable artistic licence when painting official portraits or recording state events, in a way best suited for use as propaganda. When commissioned to portray Napoleon's crossing of the Alps in the second Italian campaign of 1800, David was instructed to show the heroic *First Consul* 'calm, on a fiery horse' at the head of his men. This he accomplished with considerable style, although it was common knowledge that Napoleon had travelled on a mule, plodding along some way to the rear of the main army. Napoleon had refused even to sit for David on this occasion, telling him that it was more important to immortalise his spirit of genius than to capture his exact likeness. It was not until long after Napoleon's death that a more realistic version of the scene was painted by a Paul Delaroche (see page 142).

David favoured large-scale paintings, like his four great representations of the Imperial Coronation in 1804. These provided not only a record of the event, but were a propaganda exercise to impress on those not present in Notre Dame the solemnity and splendour of the occasion and the reality of the reconciliation between Church and State.

Napoleon Crossing the Alps by Paul Delacroche

Napoleon Crossing the Alps by Jacques-Louis David

2 The Development of the Napoleonic Legend

> **KEY ISSUES** How did the legend develop? What were its main features?

During the six years that he was on St Helena (1815–21) in the care of the British, Napoleon spent a great deal of his time perfecting his life story. From the very outset he seems to have been determined to make the most of his opportunities to justify his actions. As he pointed out to his companions, 'Our situation here may even have its attractions; the whole word is looking at us; we are martyrs in an immortal cause'. This careful re-working of his career led Tulard to conclude that 'the greatest of Napoleon's victories was over his detractors. It was at St Helena that the ogre became God'.[3] He began by dictating his own *Memoirs*, but these, concerned largely with details of his early campaigns and of Waterloo, are conspicuously dull. Much more interesting are the reminiscences, diaries and journals written by Napoleon's companions on St Helena, which record in considerable detail his conversations with them against the background of everyday life at Longwood, the house where he lived on the island.

Print of Napoleon on St Helena

The first and most influential of these documentary sources, published only a year after Napoleon' death, was the *Mémoriale de Ste Helénè*. Written by the Comte de Las Cases as a record of conversations with Napoleon between 1815 and 1818, it is probably the most important single element in the later development of the legend. Despite being described after publication as 'an effusion of sentimental old French twaddle' it sold large numbers of copies, and has been extensively, and sometimes uncritically, used ever since as the chief guide in evaluating Napoleon's own perception of his policies.

The *Mémoriale* and to some extent the journals by O'Meara (Napoleon's doctor on the island) and others need to be used with caution. They are all to some extent limited in that they were intended from the outset for publication and were written by men devoted to Napoleon. Their approach is uncritical (hagiographical, as though Napoleon were a saint) rather than balanced. (Three private journals, never meant for other eyes, present a much more unvarnished picture of Napoleon, but have only become available for study comparatively recently and have not so far been greatly used by historians and biographers.) Napoleon encouraged his companions to write down word for word everything he said, or more often dictated to them, by promising quite correctly that the records they were compiling would make their fortunes when published after his death.

Las Cases, whose *Mémoriale* runs to around 500,000 words, based his work on notes made at the time, but seems to have edited them extensively before publication, smoothing Napoleon's usual abrupt phrases and fiery rhetoric into a well-rounded literary style. Opinions vary about how accurately Napoleon's actual words were recorded by any of the diarists; but even if every word *were* reproduced exactly as spoken, 'whether it is all true is quite another thing!' as an early critic said after reading O'Meara's journal.

Did Napoleon convince himself that his version of events was correct – a case of self-deception – or did he knowingly spin the truth for political reasons – a case of intentional duplicity? No doubt, like all great men fallen from power he needed to bolster his self-esteem and justify himself to the world, to gloss over his failures, to excuse his mistakes and to explain his motives. Many historians now believe that, in the light of the political climate after 1815 – the years of the Bourbon restoration, the Holy Alliance (Austria, Prussia and Russia), and the triumph of reaction – he set out to change the public perception of his role, from that of a dictator to that of the long-time, albeit unrecognised, champion of liberalism and nationalism.

Napoleon's main aim now was to identify himself as the champion of liberalism against the reactionary monarchies of old Europe. This was the core of the Napoleonic legend. During conversations with Las Cases and the others he pointed to the liberal constitution of the Hundred Days, and declared that his previous autocratic rule had been forced upon him by circumstances, and was in any case no more than a temporary measure needed to enable him as a true patriot to defend France against her enemies. 'If I had won in 1812, my constitutional reign would have begun then. Had I reigned 20 years longer I would have shown the difference between a constitutional emperor and a king of France'. As 'the natural mediator in the struggle of the past [i.e. the old ruling families of Europe] against the Revolution' he had brought together monarchy and liberalism. He was not warlike; he had always wanted peace. It was only the old dynasties who had imposed war upon him. He had been forced to stop them destroying the Revolutionary gains in France, and to liberate and unify the peoples of Europe who were still being oppressed by feudal governments. 'Each of my victories was a diplomatic step on my road towards restoring peace to Europe ... after every victory I always offered a general peace.' If he had been given time, the 'people's Emperor' would have 'divided Europe into national states, freely formed and free internally ... a United States of Europe would have become a possibility' in a new era of peaceful economic co-operation. That he was unable to deliver his ultimate vision for Europe was in no small measure due to the opposition of Britain – paymaster of the various anti French coalitions.

After Napoleon's death in 1821 the legend gained momentum (despite an official ban until 1830 on the publication in France of any material favourable to him). Indeed, it can be argued that one of the major factors in the rapid growth of the legend in the 1820s and 1830s was Napoleon's own downfall and lonely death in exile. His carefully staged and emotional farewell to the Imperial Guard at Fontainbleau in April 1814 appealed to the poets and artists of the Romantic Age, who produced some appallingly sentimental versions of the event. Francois-René Chateaubriand, one of the outstanding French literary figures of the early nineteenth century, who had always been extremely hostile to Napoleon, pointed out how easy it was to glorify Napoleon once he was dead and his dictatorship a thing of the past:

> It is the fashion of the day to magnify Napoleon's victories. Gone are the sufferers, and the victims' curses, their cries of pain, their howls of anguish are heard to more ... no longer are parents imprisoned for their sons, nor a whole village punished for the desertion of a conscript ... no longer are the conscription lists stuck up at street corners ... It is forgotten that the people, the court, the generals, the friends of Napoleon had all become weary of his oppression and his conquests.

And people *were* forgetting that Napoleon had been a dictator, now that they were faced with life during the restoration – a dull Bourbon court, the pervasive influence of *emigrés* and priests and the end of any further glory for France. In the seeming dreariness of everyday life, the remembrance of his final defeat was forgotten and only the brilliance of his victories remained, a brilliance that seemed in retrospect to have exalted all France. The soldier, staunch republican and author Stendhal,[4] who had muttered about 'trampled liberty' and complained about imperial trappings during Napoleon's lifetime, afterwards attempted to explain why he and his contemporaries had not actively opposed Napoleon's dictatorship:

> In 1794 we had no form of religion – our spirit expressed itself in the idea of *serving our country* ... This idea *was* our religion. When Napoleon appeared [1796–7] and put an end to the series of defeats to which we were exposed by the feeble government of the Directory we considered his dictatorship solely in terms of its *military value* to France; he won victories for us and we judged all his actions by the standards of the religion which we felt in our hearts: what we valued in his dictatorship was *service being done to our country* ... Thus it was that there were men who genuinely loved Napoleon and who would admit no other criterion than that of 'serving the country' for judging the Emperor's actions.

By the 1830s the Romantics were looking back to a 'Golden Age' that never was and mourning the so-called 'martyrdom' of the last days of St Helena. O'Meara was responsible through his journal *Voice from St Helena* for adding to the legend this element of the martyr 'chained like Prometheus to a rock' or, 'Christ-like, crucified by the allies', and left there to suffer a lonely death. It is an interesting question whether, if Napoleon had been allowed to retire after Waterloo into private life in England or in the United States, as he asked permission to do, the legend would have developed and survived as it did.

A 'bored generation', born too late to have fought in his wars, found a hero in Napoleon, emphasising his conquests and the glory that he brought to France, while ignoring the deaths and the loss of political liberty that were their accompaniment. Nostalgia knew no bounds as writers began to vie with one another in fulsome adulation. Victor Hugo wrote 'The blessed poets shall kneel before you, the clouds which have obscured your glory have passed, and nothing will ever dim its true lustre again'. Novelists filled their books with idealistic young heroes whose Bible was the *Mémoriale*; cheap copies of popular and sentimental Napoleonic songs sold in their hundreds of thousands, and disaffected young men, sporting shaggy moustaches in imitation of those worn by the Imperial Guard, listened with envy to the campaign tales told by veterans of Napoleon's campaigns. It was all very Romantic and rather unreal, but the high spot was still to come.

3 The Accolade

KEY ISSUE What impact did the Napoleonic legend have?

In his will Napoleon had asked that 'my remains rest on the banks of the Seine, among the French people that I loved so well'. In a bid to court popularity, Louise-Philippe, the last king of France, decided to fulfil Napoleon's wishes and restore him to Paris. In October 1840, almost 25 years to the day since Napoleon had landed on St Helena, a French ship arrived there, with British permission, to take him home. The body, apparently untouched by time, was prepared for the long sea voyage back to France by being placed in a new coffin covered with a pall embroidered with the initial 'N' and a crown. In December the cortege arrived in Paris and with great ceremony was escorted in procession to the Invalides (a former military hospital), where the bier, surrounded by Napoleonic relics (his hat, his sword worn at Austerlitz, his insignia of the Legion of Honour), was put under the initial guardianship of a man who had enlisted as a drummer-boy in the *Grande Armée* of 1805 and had followed the Emperor ever after. With the final re-interment of the body in a magnificent sarcophagus below the dome of the Invalides, the Napoleon legend reached its high point. Hero-worship merged imperceptibly into almost religious veneration, reaching perhaps its most extreme manifestation in the late 1890s. Then, on the basis of a casual remark by Napoleon that he had the 'gift of electrifying men', he was credited by some with supernatural powers and hailed as a 'Teacher of Energy' (*Professeur d'Energie*), able 'to enlarge the souls' of those who visited his tomb.

After the death of his son, the King of Rome, in 1832 this new, uncritical version of Napoleon's career was taken up and publicised by two of his nephews. The first of these was the politically ambitious Louis-Napoleon, now head of the family (see the family tree on page 154). He staged unsuccessful *coups* in 1836 and 1840 against Louis Phillipe, in the course of which he proclaimed that he 'represented ... a principle, a cause and a defeat: the principle is the sovereignty of the people, the cause is the cause of the Empire, and the defeat is Waterloo'. The monarchy was overthrown by a revolution in 1848 and the Second Republic established. Although largely unknown, the name he shared with his illustrious uncle was certainly a factor in gaining Louis-Napoleon its Presidency. In his *Napoleonic Ideas* he set out in detail the legend view of the First Empire, describing it as an example to be followed. Louis-Napoleon seized power in 1852 and established the Second Empire. As Napoleon III he declared that he stood for 'order and authority, religion, the welfare of the people and ... for national dignity': many, therefore, expected that he would prove a reincarnation of the Napoleon of the legend. This did not happen, and with the collapse of his régime in 1870 the legend suffered an eclipse; but only temporarily. The lack of success of the Third Republic and the belief that France was being eclipsed by Germany led the legend to be revived by the second Bonaparte nephew Prince Napoleon (Jerome's son, see the Napoleonic family tree, page 154). He represents the legend in its most extreme form in which the Hero can do no wrong – 'to defend Napoleon's memory is to serve France. The glory of Napoleon is a national possession: whoever touches it defaces the nation itself'.

4 Napoleon in History

KEY ISSUE How has the study of Napoleon by historians evolved?

When news of Napoleon's death was published in London on 6 July 1821, *The Times*, an establishment newspaper, attempted an instant summary of his impact on France and Europe. It described his life as 'the most extraordinary yet known to political history'. While generously conceding that 'He was steady and faithful in his friendships, and not vindictive where it was in his power to be', the paper went on to note that:

> Buonaparte will go down to posterity as a man who ... applied his immense means to the production of a greater share of mischief and misery to his fellow-creatures, who carried on a series of aggressions against foreign states, to divert the minds of his own subjects from the sense of their domestic slavery; thus imposing on foreign nations a necessity for arming to shake off his yoke, and affording to foreign despots a pretext for following his example.[5]

Despite the view of the British, however, Napoleon never seems to have had any serious doubts about the verdict of history on his career. This was not surprising as he took great pains to provide historians with records favourable to it, both before and after 1815. It was typical of him that, glancing through old copies of the official, government sponsored newspaper, *Le Moniteur*, he expressed his approval: 'These are invariably favourable to me alone. Really talented and careful historians will write history with official documents. Now these documents are full of me; it is their testimony I solicit and invoke'.

From St Helena he attempted to pre-empt how historians might assess his life:

> I have no fear whatever about my fame. Posterity will do me justice. The truth will be known ... From nothing I raised myself to be the most powerful monarch in the world ... The historian of the Empire ... will have an easy task, for the facts speak for themselves, they shine like the sun ... On what point could I be assailed on which a historian could not defend me? For my intentions? As to these I can be absolved. For my despotism? But it can be demonstrated that dictatorship was absolutely necessary. Will it be said that I restricted liberty? It can be proved that licentiousness and anarchy still threatened liberty. Shall I be accused of being too fond of War? It can be shown I was always attacked first ... Shall I be blamed for my ambition? ... my ambition was of the highest and noblest kind that ever perhaps existed! that of establishing and consecrating the rule of reason and the exercise and enjoyment of all the human faculties! Here the historian will probably feel compelled to regret that such an ambition was not fulfilled.

Chateaubriand was one of the first critical commentators on Napoleon's career, publishing in 1814 a pamphlet denouncing him as a destroyer of men and a suppressor of freedom. Thousands of historians and writers who followed him produced works that were either 'for or against' Napoleon. Very few were neutral. Madam de Staël, whose account of Napoleon was published soon after her death in 1818, was just as critical, just as damning as Chateaubriand, but her work contains an historical perspective, setting Napoleon in his time and place, measuring him against events – and finding him wanting. In the years following his death, French histories of Napoleon multiplied rapidly. One of the most important was by Adolphe Thiers. His monumental, 20–volume work – *Histoire du Consulat et de l'Empire* – appeared between 1845 and 1862. He was deeply influenced by the Napoleonic legend, yet from a political perspective he was a liberal, who served as a minister under Louis Philippe and later embraced republicanism. Thiers had a deep dislike of the English and he much admired Napoleon's stance against them. What largely determined the approach of many nineteenth-century writers was not so much that they were 'for or against' Napoleon but that they clearly shared a belief that he had shaped the course of history. Their writings can essentially be categorised as belonging to the 'great men' school of historical study. In essence they argued that events were shaped/caused by the will of a single individual. More recently the tendency is to focus on the forces and factors that caused these dramatic events.

One of the best *résumes* of the historical debate surrounding Napoleon was by the Dutch historian Pieter Geyl, whose classic *Napoleon: For and Against*, was published in 1944. It was completed during the Nazi occupation of Holland while the author was under house arrest. Although Hitler is not mentioned in Geyl's book, he was clearly the catalyst who inspired the work. To quote Geyl

> We cannot see the past in a single communicable picture, except from a point of view, which implies a choice, a personal perspective. It is impossible that two historians, especially two living in different periods should see any historical personality in the same light. The greater the political importance of an historical character, the more impossible this is … History is indeed an argument without end.[6]

The vast addition to the literature on Napoleon could well be taken as evidence in support of this view. There remains a fascination with all aspects of the man and his life. His military achievements and campaigns in particular are an enduring source of study. Since 1945 there have been two significant developments in Napoleonic historiography.[7] Firstly there has been a shift in focus away from studying Napoleon himself to examining aspects of the way he governed his various territories. Among the issues covered by this structural approach are the way elites such as the old aristocracy and the new nobility operated, the regional responses to conscription, and issues relating to law and order under the Empire. Many of these are based on carefully researched local studies. Secondly, and possibly against a backdrop of moves towards greater European integration, there has been a move towards the wider continental experience under Napoleon. Historians have started to examine carefully the impact of Napoleonic rule on the occupied territories making up the Empire. Did these territories derive any benefits from the Empire? If so, what were they? Among the areas examined are the social structures in these territories, how they fared economically during the Empire, and what, if any, were the legacies of the French legal and administrative systems that were imposed upon them. Considerable progress has been made in understanding a wide range of issues from across the continent.

5 Conclusion: Napoleon's Legacy

KEY ISSUE What is Napoleon's legacy to France and Europe?

The personal charisma of Napoleon and the enormity of the struggle against him have assured that the periods of the Consulate and the First Empire will continue to occupy prominent positions in works on modern European history. But, once the propaganda has been stripped away and the Napoleonic legend set aside, what was his legacy to France and Europe? Some aspects of this we have already been noted (see pages 72–3) when we considered Napoleon in the context of the Revolution. Any evaluation of Napoleon's legacy for France will need to consider two areas.

First, there are the tangible changes he bequeathed to France in the field of civil life and culture. The main ones are:

- The Bank of France
- The Legion of Honour
- The Civil Code
- The prefect system
- State secondary schools
- Art and architecture – David, Arc le Triomphe, Place Vendôme Column.

Secondly, in a less tangible sense Napoleon's legacy to France is very much synonymous with *la gloire*. Admirers reflect warmly and nostalgically on the brief period when French hegemony over most of Europe was asserted and conceded. On the other hand, critics stress the baleful legacy of militarism and adventurism that continued to plague French politics intermittently for the remainder of the nineteenth century. This was only finally exorcised during the twentieth century when the threat to the survival of French society from Germany was real and immediate.

The legacy of the Empire for Europe is difficult to estimate. For the territories that France directly assimilated into the Grand Empire, there were important structural reforms to their legal and administrative systems. Yet modernisation, and wholesale dismantling of feudal structures, may well have been more apparent than real for most people. Whether life for the peasantry improved in any significant way is debatable. When the impact of the continental system and the wars are factored into the equation, then the short-term legacy for most people was one of hardship. In the longer term, Napoleon did, albeit unwittingly, help foster through his actions the forces of nationalism, particularly in Germany, Spain, Poland and Italy (see pages 106–10). His vision of a united Europe is for many an attractive proposition and in contemporary European politics appears to be slowly coming to fruition. Yet this is not a vision shard by all of Europe's citizens. In 'perfidious Albion' – as Napoleon once described Britain – opponents of further European integration still regard him as an 'ogre' and invoke his name in a pejorative way. 'Napoleon tried to submerge Britain in a single European state and he obviously wanted to abolish the pound',[8] is one of many such manifestations of this view.

Fascinated or repelled, it is impossible to stand aside, unaffected by Napoleon. He dominated an age and a continent and out-lived his death, and today the wits of historians are fully exercised in trying to unravel his life, career, impact and legacy.

References

1 See Martyn Lyons, *Napoleon Bonaparte and the Legacy of the French Revolution*, Chapter 13, 'Art, Propaganda and the Cult of the Personality' (Macmillan, 1994).
2 See Robert B. Holtman, *Napoleonic Propaganda* (Louisiana State University press, 1950).
3 J. Tulard (ed), *Napoléon à Sainte-Hélène* (Paris, 1981) p. 6.
4 Stendhal, *Vie de Napoleon* (1837).
5 *The Times*, 5 July 1821.
6 Pieter Geyl, *Napoleon: For and Against* (Penguin, 1976) pp. 15–18.
7 John Dunne, 'Napoleon: For and Against … and Beyond', *History Review* (March 1997) pp. 17–21.
8 *The Guardian*, 7 October 1999 – William Hague's conference speech to the Conservative Party.

Summary Diagram
The Growth of the Napoleonic Legend

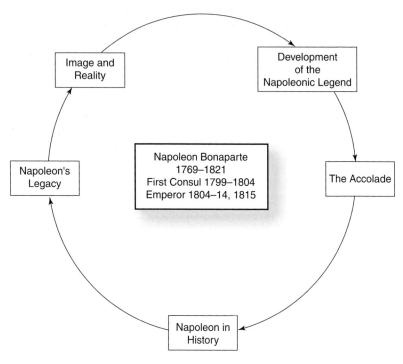

Image and Reality

Development of the Napoleonic Legend

Napoleon's Legacy

Napoleon Bonaparte
1769–1821
First Consul 1799–1804
Emperor 1804–14, 1815

The Accolade

Napoleon in History

Working on Chapter 8

This final chapter deals with a number of difficult concepts relating to the post-Napoleonic era. Two main themes are covered, namely the growth and development of the Napoleonic legend and the historiography that has emerged around the Emperor. Having read this chapter, you will begin to understand the lengths to which Napoleon went to cultivate his image. Consider carefully how he did this, firstly when in power and secondly when in exile. In your note-making, trace the emergence of the legend and what its consequences were for France. Napoleon was concerned about how he would be viewed in history and set out while in exile to try to influence those who were bound to study him. Regarding this second theme ask yourself two questions:

i) How did Napoleon *want* to be viewed in history?
ii) How *is* Napoleon viewed in history?

Source-based questions on Chapter 8

I   Read the two source on pages 145–6 and answer the following questions:

a)   How do the two sources evaluate the impact of the Napoleonic era? (*10 marks*)

b)   Why do you think the two sources provide the analysis that they give? (*15 marks*)

c)   To what extent do other sources in the chapter support either of the two views you have identified in **a**? (*20 marks*)

2   Study the two paintings on page 142 and answer the following question: What do the two paintings suggest about the use of visual propaganda and the, interpretation of events during the Napoleonic era? (*20 marks*)

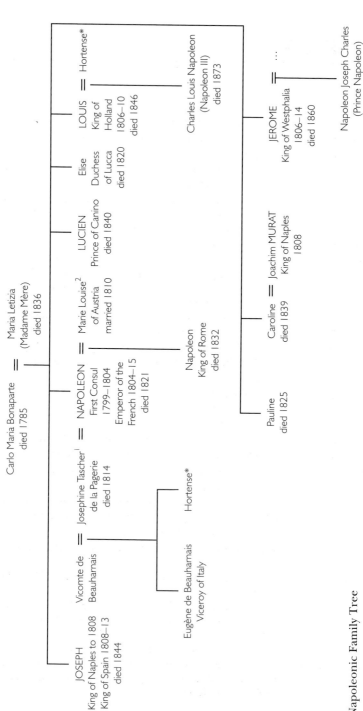

Napoleonic Family Tree

Glossary

aides	duties on food and drink
ancien régime	pre-revolutionary France – the old order
arrondissement	see *département*
biens nationaux	property of the church and *emigrés* and seized by the state and sold at auction
bourgeoisie	wealthy urban middle class (name also given by some French historians to all eighteenth-century property-owners including landowners)
commune	see *département*
coup d'etat	seizure of power by a small group of individuals
département	largest local government territorial division, made up of a collection (*arrondissement*) of communes, the smallest territorial division
domaine extraordinaire	a special fund set up in 1810 to deal with the monies levied in the conquered states
droits réunis	revised taxes on a range of goods
emigré	royalist who went into exile during the revolution
gabelle	a tax on salt
intendant	government tax official during the *ancien régime* in charge of one of France's 23 generalites
la gloire	glory, passion, patriotic fervour
lettres de cachet	written orders authorising imprisonment without trial
levée en masse	mobilisation of the whole French nation for war
livret	work permit needed by employee to obtain job
lycées	selective sate schools introduced in 1802
notables	wealthy landowners and property owners, noble and non-noble, used by Napoleon as government officials
partage	equal division of estates among male heirs
préfet	government official – successor to the intendant of the *ancien régime*
plebiscite	votes on the constitution by electors – 1800, 1802, 1804, 1815.
sans-culottes	term sometimes applied to all poorer classes but more applicable to urban craftsmen, traders and small shop-keepers
senatorerie	estate and revenues granted to a favoured senator
senatus consultum	procedure adopted in 1801 allowing the senate to issue constitutional changes bypassing the legislature, effectively rule by decree

Further Reading

There are thousands of books on Napoleon, his empire and France in 1799–1815, the majority in French, but with an expanding number in English or available in translation. The following is a small selection from this vast collection.

Access books that complement this one are **Dylan Rees and Duncan Townson**, *France in Revolution* (Hodder & Stoughton, 2001) and **Neil Stewart**, *The Changing Nature of Warfare 1700–1945* (Hodder & Stoughton, 2001).

Many single volume biographies of Napoleon have been published over the years. Among the long established volumes, the following are worth noting: **J.M. Thompson**, *Napoleon* (Blackwell, 1952); **F. Markham**, *Napoleon* (Weidenfeld and Nicolson, 1963); and **G. Lefebvre**, *Napoleon* (Paris, 1935, English translation Routledge and Kegan Paul, 1969) and *Napoleon: From Tilsit to Waterloo* (Routledge, 1969) – works of an eminent Marxist historian, they are despite their age classics. **V. Cronin**, *Napoleon* (Collins, 1971), provides a pleasant 'easy-read' introduction to the subject for both student and general reader. **J. Tulard**, *Napoleon – the Myth of the Saviour* (Paris, 1977, English translation Weidenfeld and Nicolson, 1984), although not strictly speaking a biography, is full of thought-provoking ideas about the role of the saviour figure in French history. **I. Collins**, *Napoleon: First Consul and Emperor of the French* (Historical Association, 1986) is a pamphlet which provides a stimulating introductory overview. Among the recent crop of biographies the following contain excellent analysis of his career, combined with much recent research – **R.S. Alexander**, *Napoleon* (Arnold, 2001), **Alexander Grab**, *Napoleon and the Transformation of Europe* (Palgrave, 2003) and **Geoffrey Ellis**, *Napoleon* (Longman, 1997). No list would be complete without **P. Geyl**, *Napoleon: For and Against* (Cape, 1949), a detailed comparative study of French historians' views on Napoleon.

For Napoleon's domestic policies the following are particularly useful: **Hubert Cole**, *Fouché, The Unprincipled Patriot* (Eyre & Spottiswoode, 1971); **Malcolm Crook**, *Napoleon Comes to Power: Democracy and Dictatorship in Revolutionary France, 1795–1804* (University of Wales Press, 1998) which also contains a selection of sources; **Martyn Lyons**, *Napoleon Bonaparte and the Legacy of the French Revolution* (Macmillan, 1994); and **L. Bergeron**, *France Under Napoleon* Paris (1972, English translation Princeton, 1981), which covers social, cultural and economic affairs based on the author's own substantial research.

Far more books relating to Napoleon and Europe have been written. The following are recommended: **C. Barnett**, *Napoleon* (Allen and Unwin, 1978) is a well-illustrated volume by a military historian which focuses on this aspect of Napoleon's activities; **Michael Broers**, *Europe Under Napoleon 1799–1815* (Arnold, 1996); **G. Ellis**, *Napoleonic Empire* (Macmillan, 1991); **Charles J. Esdaile**, *The French Wars 1792–1815* (Routledge, 2001); and **D.M.G. Sutherland**, *France 1789–1815: Revolution and Counter Revolution* (Fontana, 1985). **D.G. Wright**, *Napoleon and Europe* (Longman, 1984), provides a general introduction to Napoleon and his European Empire, together with a few selected documents. For those interested in military campaigns Charles Esdaile's *The Peninsular War* (Penguin, 2003) is both detailed and absorbing.

A number of English-language documentary collections are available to students. Among those largely concerned with Napoleon's own words, whether spoken or written, are **S. de Chair** (**ed**), *Napoleon's Memoirs* (Faber and Faber, 1948); **Philip G. Dwyer and Peter McPhee (eds)**, *The French Revolution and Napoleon: A Sourcebook* (Routledge, 2002); and **J.M. Thompson** (**ed**), *Napoleon's Letters* (Dent, 1954). Two works which consider the campaigns from the perspectives of those directly involved are **C. Hibbert** (**ed**), *A Soldier of the 71st* (Leo Cooper, 1975) and **A. Brett-James** (**ed**), *Eyewitness Accounts of Napoleon's Defeat in Russia* (Macmillan, 1966).

Index